The Black Do

Belmont, Lancashire

New Route Book

Compiled and edited by

Phil Kelly

This volume introduced by

Ian Lonsdale

ISBN: 9798389142404

Imprint: Independently published

v1.01

First edition: 2023

Table of Contents

The Black Dog

Series Overview

Welcome to climbing history – in the raw!

As a young climber in the 1980s I was always fascinated when we were able to read the books that had been left in various locations; reading the first ascent records in the words of the climbers who actually did the climbing, in their own handwriting and often signed. It made the whole thing so close and so personal.

Climbing new routes is indeed a personal thing. Each one is a unique journey that only the first ascensionist can experience, and completely different on each and every one.

That personal experience and connection with the route is often laid bare in the handwritten records in the new route books and is a probably the clearest example of climbing history 'in the raw'.

Those books were the basis for communication and debate, and fed the contents of forthcoming guidebooks, well before the deployment of more modern-day internet grade and quality voting algorithms.

Apart from the factual contents of these books though there is often an ongoing underlying narrative that was never written down or described as such, but reading them, one can sense the times, the passions, competition and controversies. These are often tales which have never been told, and probably a lot of them will never be told, but that's all part of the mystery and the reasons for publishing the books in this format.

RockArchivist

The RockArchivist project started in earnest back in 2009 when I moved to Sheffield and started to think more about the opportunities almost on my doorstep.

I tracked down the custodian of the surviving Stoney Café routes books and agreed that they could be published. Then I did the same with the Outside in Hathersage and started to cast the net wider.

The late Pete Norton (of Pete's Eats Café fame) embraced the idea immediately and gave permission for whatever we needed to do, which saw me driving over to Llanberis to pick up a huge plastic box containing all the surviving books from the café from the new owner, Tom Potter.

Lover's Leap Café, Stoney Middleton, 1982

Whilst in Wales I then drove over to Eric Jones' house and agreed exactly the same with Eric, so we had the Snowdonia range covered quite early on and would be followed later with the books from Lyon Sports in Llandudno, detailing the developments of the limestone crags on the Ormes.

Brian Cropper was massively keen to get his archives digitised, especially his new route books from the YHA in Manchester, and these would later be joined by three books from Rock 'n Run in Ambleside, the lost book from Tanky's shop in Sheffield, Joe Royle's shop in Buxton, and the book which really started it for me; the Black Dog book, which was still kept by Ian Lonsdale and brought back innumerable memories.

Overall, there are over 10,000 scanned pages in the RockArchivist collection, and it is hoped that we can work through these to now publish them in hard copy book format for everyone to enjoy in (almost) their original format. The collection is also still growing, and if possible new volumes will be released when the opportunity allows.

For now though, I hope you enjoy browsing these books in their native form. You might even get out a biro and write your own comments, but above all, just enjoy browsing.

Acknowledgements

Thanks must be given to Ian Lonsdale for his excellent introduction to this volume. For anyone active in the quarries during the period covered by the Black Dog book, Ian's comments should invoke some wonderful memories.

Thanks also to everyone who recorded their developments in the book, those who provided constructive comments and responses, and those who led in any way to the book being the wonderful magnifying glass on the County's climbing history that it is.

To all the owners and guardians of new route books that have embraced the RockArchivist project and agreed to us preserving these in digital format for future generations to view; thank you one and all!

A Note on Royalties

The original plan for RockArchivist was for it to be a completely non-profit project, and I am proud to say that this is still the case.

A portion of nett profits from the books in the RockArchivist new route book series will be used in support of a variety of causes, from local mountain rescue teams, the North Wales bolt fund, preserving the raw historical record for future generations, and maintaining the climbers' memorial area in Wilton One (Lancashire).

Your support for these causes by purchasing the new routes volumes is gratefully received by all concerned, so thank you for this support.

Future Publications

If you have, or aware of any other new route books and think that they should be made available to climbers in the same way that this book and the rest in the series have been done, feel free to contact us to arrange, by email at: rockarchivist@outlook.com.

Phil Kelly, June 2023

Volumes in the RockArchivist Collection

Stoney Café 1982

Stoney Café 1985

Stoney Café 1985

Stoney Café 1986

Stoney Café 1987

Stoney Café 1988

Stoney Café 1990

Stoney Café 1991-1996

Black Dog 1981-1985

Brian Cropper

The Outside 1987-2001

The Outside 2001-2009

Outside 2009-2023

Pete's Eats 1978-1983

Pete's Eats 1983-1985

Pete's Eats 1985

Pete's Eats 1985

Pete's Eats 1986

Pete's Eats 1987

Pete's Eats 1988

Pete's Eats 1988	Pete's Eats 1989	Pete's Eats 1989	Pete's Eats 1989	Pete's Eats 1990
Pete's Eats 1991	Pete's Eats 1992	Pete's Eats 1992	Pete's Eats 1994	Pete's Eats 1995
Pete's Eats 1995	Pete's Eats 1997	Pete's Eats 2002-2009	Tremadog 1984	Tremadog 1988

Tremadog 1991	Tanky's Shop 1975-1979	Rock 'n Run Book 1	Rock 'n Run Book 2	Rock 'n Run Book 3

Joe Royle's Book 1	Joe Royle's Book 2	Lyon Sports	Moorland Rambler

About this Volume – Ian Lonsdale

I moved into the Black Dog in May 1980 and it quickly became the epicentre of Lancashire climbing.

Thursdays became the traditional meeting nights, where plans for the weekend were made and trips organised; there was a very buoyant atmosphere of storytelling and mickey taking that made those evenings very special with the occasional lock in! Allegedly.

In the winter months, Black Pudding Team dinners were held, as well as guest lectures and slide shows. Some well-known names came along including Don Whillans who became a regular, Al Rouse, John Cleare and Martin Boysen to name a few. Impromptu parties and more impromptu parties were the norm. The Black Dog scene lasted five years and packed in so many memories.

It wasn't until 1981 that the Black Dog new routes book came into being, and this was by chance, rather than going to YHA in Manchester, where better than and more local than the Black Dog to have its own new route book?!

New route books are unique time capsules of historical events as they happen: raw information, thoughts and experiences, written down blow-by-blow for all to see and comment on, and boy did they get commented on!

Also, occasional 'phantom' routes would be recorded as massive mickey takes, all in the name of fun, obviously.

One entry, Friday the 18th May 1984, Mark Leach and Phil Kelly came into the Black Dog with Mark having completed the first ascent of one of the last great problems at Wilton, if not the whole of Lancashire - the iconic 'S-shaped Groove' in Wilton Two.

This was a colossal moment in Lancashire rock climbing history about to be recorded in the Black Dog new route book.

Sat facing the fire in the snug, pen at the ready, book open, Mark started the recording of a momentous first ascent, *"what you are going to call it?"* I asked in trepidation.

Ian Lonsdale behind the bar
Photo: Brian Cropper

Then Phil blurted: PANGALACTICGARGLEBLASTER !!! (all one word). *"What the F...!"* was my reaction, *"you're not going to call one of the last great problems of Lancashire that."* In desperation and for inspiration I went to the juke box, whilst Mark wrote the name and description in the book.

Scrolling though the list of songs on the juke box I saw a Phil Collins song, big at the time - *"Against all Odds."*

"Right, this is what you're going to call it..." I said in a controlled and persuasive manner, getting Mark to scribble out and replace the offending name.

It's only recently that I've been told that *"Pan Galactic Gargle Blaster"* is a drink from the Douglas Adams book, *The Hitchhiker's Guide to the Galaxy*, described as *"like having your brains smashed out by a slice of lemon, wrapped 'round a large gold brick."* And there's me thinking it was some made up joke!

When the reader goes through this record of first ascents in Lancashire, and indeed new route books from other areas, you need to be reminded that this was still in the era of snail mail and slow communication, and these books became the essential record for guidebook writers and magazines to tap into.

9AM and still going strong. Longridge Crazy Gang members in the Black Dog
Photo: Andrew Gridley collection

As Lancashire climbing evolved, there became a scarcity of any recorded history, unlike say the Peak District, Lake District or Wales, that had active climbing clubs whose histories extended back into the very early 1900s when the art of rock climbing as we know it was born.

The first rock climbing guidebook to be published in the Peak District was in 1913, titled *'Some Short Climbs in Derbyshire and Elsewhere'*, by John Laycock. The first rock climb guide to the Lake District was published in 1922 and in Wales 1909. To achieve these and subsequent guidebooks for these areas there has been a steady flow of factual information from new routes books and climbing club journals in the respective areas.

The first guidebook for Lancashire didn't appear until 1969, there had been some guides privately published to the Wilton Quarries, Hoghton, and for Brownstones and Cadshaw Rocks in the LC&CC club journal but with little or no recorded first ascent information.

We know that climbing had been taking place in the quarries as early as the mid-1930s but again with no records, so it's always been word of mouth, and open to interpretation.

The Black Dog new routes book was the first of its kind in Lancashire to openly record first ascents, by the first ascensionists. This eventually led to the first ascent list in the 1999 guide Lancashire Rock (AKA The Brick), but even this was only accurate from the 1980s onward, and thanks partly to the Black Dog new route book.

So, I hope you enjoy this record of a little moment in time, and thank you for supporting this publication, whose nett profits will maintain the memorial area in Wilton One, remembering those who have left us, whilst at the same time remembering the times they shared with us.

Ian Lonsdale, June 2023

The Wilton One Climbers' Memorial Area

The climbers' memorial area, located on the picturesque hillside opposite the Prow's outside face, was created in 2017 by volunteers, giving climbers and visitors a place for reflection and remembrance of climbing friends and family who have sadly passed.

Besides its original purpose, it is also a convenient place to take some time out from a day's cragging, to sit around for lunch, to share tales, and to generally relax away from the crag.

Being located where it is, the memorial area is frequently also visited by local youths, who may not be quite as respectful as we would like. Monies raised from this publication will be used to support ongoing maintenance activities so that we can continue to use this area as it was designed.

WILTON ONE

Shaggy Dog   XS 5c (E4) ✓

Swing Ⓛ from base of Kettle Crack
and mantle onto a ledge. P.R.
Step Ⓒ and climb the wall boldly
to the top

19/7/81

Hank Pasquill
Paul Clark

ANGLEZARKE.

Please Lock Me Away _ XS 6b/c (E4)

The obvious undercut flake and crack line
between Klondyke and Gates of Perception.

Bernie Bradbury _ unseconded _ 26/6/81

E4 6c or more Rock-Cock

WILTON TWO

PIGS ON THE WING   E4 6B (45FT)

CLIMBS THE WALL BETWEEN SWINE AND
WILTON WALL. FINISHING JUST LEFT OF
SWINE. RUNNERS PLACED LEVEL WITH THE
FLAKE ON WILTON WALL TO PROTECT THE
LOWER (CRUX) WALL

JOHN HARTLEY
21ST JULY '81
(SECOND DID NOT FOLLOW)

WILTON THREE.

CRACKED ORANGE' 30FT H.V.S. 5A.

CLIMB THE WALL DIRECT JUST LEFT OF ORANGE
CRACK WITHOUT USING THE CRACK OR LEDGES ON
THE LEFT.
JOHN HARTLEY (E00)?

1

CONCRETE CRACK   HMS

CLIMBS THE OBVIOUS CRACK STARTING 7' up
and to Left of ~~Concrete~~ Cement Mix, to finish up
that Route

E3 6a

more like E2 5c
M leads

HOW COME YOU COULDN'T DO IT
FIRST TIME THEN!

How come you couldn't do it 1st time either
(P.R)

IAN LONSDALE
Andy Moss.

2

ANGLEZARKE QUARRY

1 TANGERINE TRIP   E6 6C   FA. J.CRENSHAW
                                  J.HOUSEDALE JULY

2 GROND.   HVS 5A?   FA?

3 PG   HARF   E1 5B   FA. J.CRENSHAW
                                  J.HOUSEDALE JU?

<u>CADSHAW QUARRY</u>

'ON THE ROAD AGAIN'   75'   H.V.S.   5a/b.

Climbs the obvious thin crack on the buttress immediately right
of the mineshaft starting up a v-groove.
    F.A. Tony Brindle
       Gary McCarthy   28ᵗʰ May.

WILTON ONE

~~RAINY DAYS & MONDAYS~~ U.P.   E4   6B
      FORMERLY SHAKE
CLIBIB CRACK ABOVE FRIGHTFUL FRE
   LEDGE. ~~VERY~~ STRENUOUS
     FAIRLY ~~a~~ ONE POINT OF RESI.
      G⁽ᵉᵒꜰ⁾ MANN   NOT AID.
      N. BONNETT   14/7/81
       'IGEL

<u>EGERTON QUARRY</u>

<u>CEREMONY - 35' - VS 4C</u>
   FOLLOW THE OBVIOUS LINE JUST L. OF WET DREAMS.
   GOOD CLIMBING.
    NIGEL HOLMES
    TONY PRESTON
    DEAN HARRIS   APRIL 81.

<u>LIFE DURING WARTIME - 60' - HVS 5A</u>
FOLLOW AMPHITHEATRE TERRACE TO THE GRASSY BAY
AND AN ANCIENT PEG. CLIMB UP AND R. IN LARGE
HOLDS TO A TRAVERSE R. TO THE BASE OF A THIN CRACK
FINISH UP THIS. (PR REMOVED)
   JOHN MONKS
   NIGEL HOLMES
   CHRIS FLETCH   JUNE 81.

<u>NASTY LITTL</u>   HVS - 4B/4A
FROM THE   L.H.S   of   LY WALL CLIMB THE LICHE OVERLAP
   PAST A PIR T   B EXNTICIPATING LEDGE AN   UIG TRA
      TO   UP A GROOVE SE IOUS

WILTON TWO

157 Short Corner A1 Now H.V.S 5A
PSL Protection Removed

Ian Lonsdale 17th April 81 ✓
John Fitton

WILTON ONE.

CLAPPED OUT A2 NOW X5 5c E3 6A

JOHN MONKS 23rd APRIL ✓
MICK BLOOD

EGERTON QUARRY

GUILLOTINE HVS 5b ✓

John Monks   Finger crack & peapod to right
Mick Blood   of athelred.
Nige Holmes

STANWORTH. QUARRY
                                    (X5)
FUCHS ACROSS THE POLE   HVS 5C.

SOUTH POLE BUTTRESS
START AT RIGHT END OF BUTTRESS TRAV
WITH DIFFICULTY AND FINISH UP SHORT GROOVE

D. CRENSHAW   APRIL 87.

J. RYDEN   NOT ME
L. K. AINSWORTH
          MAYBE.

PTO

ADRENERLIN   EX   1 PT RESTING

H. PASQUI ✓
l Lonsdale

1ˢᵗ Aug 81.

Augbi   FREE H. Parquill.
G Mann

K.P

.R   2ᴺᴰ Act   D. Hall . 7ᵗʰ Sept 81.

confermed its 6 D. Grade   dispensed with R
pond

3ᴿᴰ Act   P. KIRTON

WILTON ONE

✓ SILENTLY SCREAMING 45FT E4 6B. ✳✳

(CLIMBS THE ARETE RIGHT OF DEODAND)

START IN THE SHORT CORNER RIGHT OF THE ARETE. CLIMB
UP UNTIL ~~IT IS PO~~ A TRAVERSE LEFT TO THE ARETE CAN
BE MADE. STRAIGHT UP THE ARETE TO FINISH. (2 PEG RUNNERS)
PEG BELAY. (TRAVERSE OFF RIGHT).

More like E3 6a
Tim Lowe.

JOHN HARTLEY
PAUL CLARK (DOCTOR BOB)
MARK KEMBALL.
14/8/82.

FOOL'S PARADISE (SEVERE) LESTER MILL (SET BACK)
25'

5' left of PC2 – Major crack line with loose spike.
Climb 15' to ledge. Finish up short wall.

DAVE SANDERSON.
ROGER BUNYAN.
18/8/82.

LESTER MILL 'Set back'

Juggernaut
        Start as for "Hit By A LORRY" up to ledge.
Climb lower bulging arete and step into niche on face.
Climb face direct to finish. Poor protection on crux moves.
        V.S. 4b 30ft.

23.8.82   Dave Sanderson.
Second did not follow due to marathon
stress.

Wilton One   26/8/82.

✓ Fist Finish H.V.S. 5b   (~~~~ to Knuckleduster)
  From the belay ledge of Knuckleduster, climb the thin
crack behind the ledge, continuing up the wall ~~above~~ to finish
on the hanging flake.
        Mark Kemball, Ian Lonsdale, John Hartley.

LESTER MILL   (Set Back)

"Resolute Roc"   V.S. 4b   35'
                            ~~30~~

      8' Left of 'Hit By A Lorry'. Climb flake
  crack to ledge. Then climb slightly
  overhanging face direct * using crack, to
  finish.
        Roger Bunyan   1/9/82.
        Dave Sanderson

WILTON ONE

✓   THE DEVILS ALTERNATIVE   55Ft. E4 6B * *

(START 8Ft LEFT OF DEODAND)
    CLIMB UP TO THE OVERHANG. PULL OVER AND CLIMB
THE WALL ABOVE USING TWO SHALLOW GROOVES, TO A
HORIZONTAL BREAK. TRAVERSE RIGHT TO PEG BELAY ON
SILENTLY SCREAMING.
                    .
                        JOHN HARTLEY
                        PAUL CLARK (?)
                        2/9/82

WILTON ONE

✓   TWICE REMOVED FROM YESTERDAY 45Ft E1 5B *

FREECLIMBS PROLINE.
                        CHRIS RONSON
                        KEITH HARRISON
                        2/9/82

    Not Valid if   (CLIMBED BY TONY PRESTON)
  not documented   →   4-5 YEARS AGO

9

Storey   Where is this crag?

St. Paul E2 5b/c

Climb the wall right of St. Peter Pa
over a small overlap, then straight up.
A surprisingly good route.
P. Cropper N. Siddiqui D. Campell 24/7/82

HOGHTON.

HIGHWAY STAR - FREE at 5b.

WHEN THE LEVEE BREAKS - FREE 5a, 5b, 5c, 5b, 4c, 4c.

WILTON ONE

ASTRADYNE 40 FT E4 6B ***

CLIMBS THE THIN BULGING CRACK 15FT LEFT OF
PARADOX TO A LEDGE BELOW THE TOP. PEG BELAY
ROUND THE CORNER ON THE LEFT. (IT IS BEST TO ABSEIL OFF)

                    JOHN HARTLEY
                    JOHN MONKS
                    2/8/82

LESTER MILL. QUARRY
   "Hit By A Lorry."
Left of Kink at bottom of rubble cone large
crack with chockstones - climb direct through
two ledges finish by loose arete. 40ft Hard
Severe.
       Roger Bunyan
       Dave Sanderson.   5/6/82

"Lancashire Crumbly" left left of about KLINK

   climb slab via scoop direct to ledge - step
right 2ft finish up to KLINK to lei above lei 45ft. Hard Severe
            R. Bunyan. 5/6/82

WILTON TWO

LAYING THE GHOST 25FT E3 6B   E2

(FREE CLIMBS PHANTOM 'A1')

CLIMB THE CORNER FOR A FEW FEET AND SWING OUT
LEFT UP THE CRACK (P.R.)

JOHN HARTLEY
JOHN MONKS
25.5.82.

WILTON TWO

THE WASP 30FT E3 6A.

CLIMB THE SHORT ARETE RIGHT OF THE BEE TO A LEDGE.
CLIMB UP USING THE THIN CRACK IN THE RIB ABOVE.

JOHN HARTLEY
JOHN MONKS
26.5.82.

WILTON TWO

THE DISAPPEARING ACES   (E formerly ace of Spades)   E36a.

CLIMB THE GROOVE LEFT OF THE CRACK OF ACE OF SPADES

DENIS GLEESON
JOHN MONKS   26.5.82.

EGERTON   NOBODY WEPT FOR ALEC TRENCH.
E4 6A.

Climbs the striking arete right of
chalk lightening crack. 2 Pegs preplaced.
serious.   Top-roped prior to ascent.
DAI LAMPARD
NIGEL HOLMES.   27/5/82

WILTON TWO

DANCERS AT THE END OF TIME E4 6B

① 20FT 5C.
START UNDER SATURDAY CRACK, AND TRAVERSE LEFT
TO THE ARETE PEG BELAY.

② 60FT 6B.
CONTINUE TRAVERSING LEFT AT THE SAME HEIGHT,
CROSSING WILTON WALL, FALLING CRACK AND
FINISHING UP BIG DORRI'S.

JOHN HARTLEY ②
JOHN MONKS ①
28·5·82.

WILTON ONE

POT POURRI V.S. 4b 60'

10 feet right of Gooty Muckden. Climb directly up the
wall via a vague groove to the break. Finish direct.
DENIS GLEESON 29/5/82
(Solo.)

WILTON TWO

SAVAGE STONE 25FT E4 7A.

CLIMB 'DIRECT' FOR A FEW FEET AND SWING LEFT
INTO THE HANGING GROOVE. CLIMB THIS WITH ONE
PEG RUNNER

MAYBE 6C 6a IT IS FUCK OFF

JOHN HARTLEY
2·6·82
SECOND DID NOT FOLLOW
(TWAS KNACKERED)

MUST BE A BETTER CLIMBER THAN PAULSON ANYWAY WHO EVEN THOUGH THOUGHT IT E4.

GOT IT IN ONE

Phil Kelly

HOW DO YOU KNOW BEING DRAGGED ON THE END OF A ROPE?

WILTON 1

TYRANNOSAURUS FREE E4 6B

MARK LEACH
DAVE KENYON
CRUISED IT.

No End Paul did it I want it

I LED IT IN BETTER STYLE
than 2 ascents it's had that seen

Hog Houghton Quarry.

SPIDER RIDER.   E4 6C.   THIS ROUTE IS NOW NUKED!
Over hanging crack right of Wasp 3 pegs   ledge
① 60 ft 6C overhang crock sustained. to small ledge
② 40 ft 5B climb crack for 10 ft then traverse out
right & and finish up an arête.

        Mark Leach + Ian Conway

            May 82.

Any Resting On Runners? Mark? —phil

COWS MOUTH QUARRY.

DAYTONA WALL.   NewBolt Placed by Abseil
                     (NOT ME—▬▬▬▬).
A lead of this Route is Now possible, Thanks to
the Phantom Bolter @ ▬6a. E3.

                Phil Kelly

                        E2 5C PP ← WOU

DEEPLY VALE MEIN KAMPF free E3 6a.

Yes, you know it is, but were the 3 Bolts + 1 peg not.
Declared ~That Leach guy again.

            HOGHTON QUARRY.
THE EXCITABLE BOY.   E4 6b.
    THE CRACK LEFT OF ?   (POSSIBLY CANDLEMASS FREE)
        THE KENYON + HIS FOLLOWER.   FEB '93.

WILTON 1
    FALLING WALL 35FT E1 5b.
        Wall 20ft left of Willow Arête E,
            Takes the thin crack to small ledge then
    directly up the wall above.

    not a very good Route (PK)   Tim Lowe
                                 Dave Vose 19/5/83.

WILTON 1

THE POWER OF THE MEKON   30ft   E1 5C
THE WALL LEFT OF GROVEL TRENDING R.

DAVE   WILLIAMS
Paul   HEATON

THE VETERAN COSMIC ROCKER   25'   E3 6B
sustained
The   R   Arête   of   Flytrap.   start   below
the   triangular   roof   and   climbed   to   its   left.
ruing   round   the   arête   on   insecure Pinches
and   lieback   its   R   hand   side.

It   25ft   HVS 5B
The   wall   L   of   This
both   Mark Leach   and   solo

~~CRAITOR   T.~~   E6a 2nd Asc. PR
CRATER   TRAITOR   80ft   ~~E5~~ 6a   serious !!!
~~serious~~ ~~████~~
The   wall   R   of   Goon .   Starting   in
a   shallow   groove ,   climb   direct   to   a
RURP !   move   up   and   R   to   a   PR   then
back   L   where   hard   moves   lead   to
the   top .   Traverse   R   over   the   crap
where   you   can   lower   of   the   sapling
~~████████████████████████████████~~
~~████████████████████████████████~~
Paul   Pritchard
Gaz   Mc~~ander~~lish

PLENTY OF ZZZZ's *** E3 5C

Pitch 1 (or Pitch of grey & white) From last Pitch of grey & white girdle Traverse into clapped out via the slab of blackout. Belay on peg & friends.

Pitch 2 (8) DO MASTER spy roof and traverse onto Jug on black MAMBA. (Arrange Pro[it is possible to rest in groove]). Then R to PR on SHAGGY DOG. Continue R to a belay on the rusty bar which holds up the whole buttress R of kettle crack. Rap off. AN EXCELLENT Pitch better than the rest of grey and white girdle. Too right (AdB)

ANGLZARKE

THE CHANGEing E1 5B 40 ft
SUSED NOT A VERY ORIGINAL NAME

FREE CLIMB'S (TORROWEAP OVER LOOK.) GRAND CANYON

GREG RIMMER : THE MOTION PICTURE E4 5C/6a
Jimmy up slanting crack and follow its continuation flake till it is possible to go left into a groove and power up to a ledge. go L again and finish up overloin.

COWSMOUTH Quarry
DAYTONA WALL Direct start 6b
makes the rout E4

Alias Phil Kelly (solo)

15

Lester Mill Quarry.

Whip Me! Whip Me!   Severe   20'

Top of grass covered cone left of "Twin Grooves".
Climb right crack and top then over blocks.
Top loose.
                        5 ⬛/9/82   R. Bunyan
                                            D. Sanderson.

Anglezarke.
    The Rapidity of Sleep.   E2   6b.   80'

    Gains and climbs the thin flake crack right
of "Flake Out". Led with pre-placed nut, then
soloed. Abseil from a ledge 10' from top to
avoid certain death.
                        Aug 82   Mark Liptrot
                    "Second did not try to follow."

Obiwan   60'   E2   6a.

    Free climbs the old aid route "Havasupai". This
grade takes into account peg protection which
someone has subsequently removed. Abseil off.
                        Aug '82   Mark Liptrot.

WILTON 1

~~FINE~~

GRASSLEARSE   DONE BEFORE
                     VS 4c AS JOHN HARTLEY'S
                                   MEGA
                                   BOLT
                                   ROUTE
                                   E76a

~~BETWEEN GRASS AND WILLOW~~
~~WALL. DIRECT UP THE SLAB ON~~
~~RUGOSITIES DIRECT TO THE LAWN ON~~
~~A LEDGE~~

~~GRIDS (Second (John Margesten) did~~
~~not follow. actuar~~
~~fell asleep with boredom)~~

Grids
This route is Brilliant, Honest.
                    Phil

LEICESTER MILLS

"RETURN TO FANTASY" E2 5c 70' *

Start to left of Rumper at obvious corner with pedestal ledge at 15'. Climb the obvious corner crack line with increasing difficulty, final 10' of which could be avoided by taking edge on the right. Good belays on tree to left & big block to right.

Dave Cronshaw Greg Rimmer
25-8-83.

"BRILLIANT ROUTE" MIKE FAULKNER.

"THE BEAST" E3 5c/6a 85' ***
Start just left of Evil Crystal, move left beneath overhang & up bearing left to obvious niche. Gain niche with difficulty. Exit direct via tree hold, very thin

Dave Cronshaw / John Ryden
1.9.83.

ATTERMIRE. "WHO'D A THOWT IT?" E2 5c
100 FT.
A DIRECT LINE UP GORGON BUTTRESS TO THE BULGE. OVER THIS AND UP THE FINELY SITUATED GROOVE ABOVE. BEST LINE AT ATTERMIRE.

TONY BRINDLE ERIC DEARDEN
28/8/83.

DENHAM. "CYCLOPS" HVS 5A. 35FT.

STRAIGHT UP OVER THE OVERHANG BELOW
THE OBVIOUS EYE 16 YDS RIGHT OF GREEN CRACK
CLIMB TO THE TOP VIA TWO MANTLES.

ERIC DEARDEN. SOLO.

Reddyshore Scout

Nº4 Test Piece Free. E1 5C

John Stanger M Harrison
May 1983

THE TEST PIECE WOULD APPEAR TO
BE AN INABILITY TO WRITE STRAIGHT
AND BETWEEN LINES.

LEICESTER MILL
(EVIL WALL)

MIXED VEG FREE HVS 5b

ALSO DIRECT START UP OVERHANGING.
GROOVE.

~~HS 5b~~ DAVE CRONSHAW. SOLO
E1 5b   12-9-83.   ME

DENHAM.

BULLWORKER   E3 6a

Climbs Former aid route Torradus using 9
3 situ peg runners. Please do not remove
pegs as custom made & took all day to place.
28.6.82 Dave Cronshaw. John Ryden + Sutherin

'Top peg runner has been removed! Why?

WILTON !

ROLL OVER DIRECT.   NOW E2

Cause D.C. says so. Wipeout still E1

EGERTON   QUARRY.

BAG OF BONES   50' HVS 4c

climbs obvious crackline starting from ledges just L. of
Wednesday Corner.
Geoff Mann, Nigel Holmes, Dai Lampard.

NIFF-NIFF THE GUINEA PIG - 50' - E2 5b

An elimante line climbing the wall R. of Gallows Pole.
Dai Lampard, Nigel Holmes, Chris Fletcher.

EACH-WAY NUDGER - 40' - HVS.
The overhung corner 50' L. of the start to Amphitheatre
Terrace. Technical.

Direct Start to 10 minutes before the Worm. HVS 5b

Mike Bullough (Solo)   Bag of shit.

STANWORTH

SPACE BUTTRESS

GRAVITY WELL G3 6b

A DIRECT LINE THROUGH A POCKET AT
15' JUST R. OF APOLLO.

> Dave Kenyon. Make Haslam
> Greg Rimmer.

ARM STRONG H.V.S. 5c

A DIRECT START TO THE L.H. POCKET
OF APOLLO, STARTING AT A SMALL LEDGE

> Haslam, Mick Ryan, Rimmer

MOONRAKER H.V.S. 5c

A DIRECT LINE UP THE L.H.S. OF
THE APOLLO WALL.

> Make + Mike Haslam.

EXPLORER'S BUTTRESS

LIVERPOOL DOCS H.V.S. 5c

THE SLAB BETWEEN THE R.H. ARÊTE
AND COLUMBUS.

> John Noblett.

NORTH POLE BUTTRESS

ENERGY VAMPIRE H.V.S. 5c

A CONTRIVED LINE BETWEEN PEARY
AND NANSEN, STARTING UP A CRACK. (I.P.R.)

> Noblett, Ryan.

THE EQUATOR

FLOOD GATE E1 5c

AN OBVIOUS CRACK ABOUT 30' L. OF
TROPICAL CORNER.

> Kenyon, Haslam.

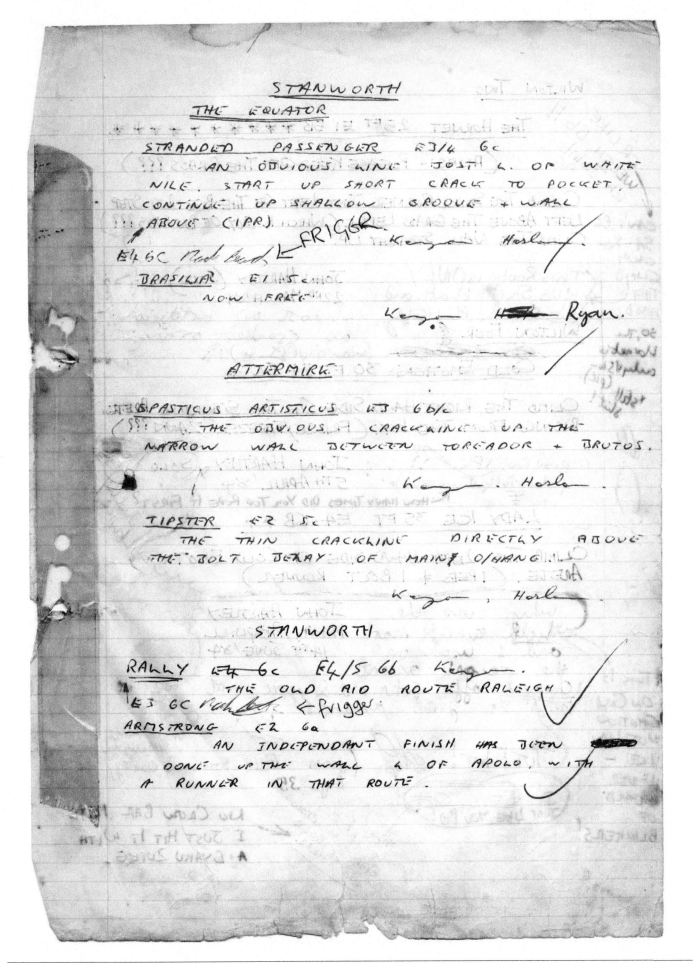

STANWORTH

THE EQUATOR

STRANDED PASSENGER E3/4 6c
AN OBVIOUS LINE JUST L. OF WHITE
NILE. START UP SHORT CRACK TO POCKET,
CONTINUE UP SHALLOW GROOVE + WALL
ABOVE (1PR).

E4 6C *Rock head* ←FRIGGR   *Kenya & Harlow.*

BRASILIA *...last...*
NOW *HERE...*

    Kenyo ~~Harlow~~ Ryan.

ATTERMIRE

SPASTICUS ARTISTICUS E3 6b/c
THE OBVIOUS CRACKLINE UP THE
NARROW WALL BETWEEN TOREADOR + BRUTOS.

    Kenyo . Harlow .

TIPSTER E2 5c E4 5c
THE THIN CRACKLINE DIRECTLY ABOVE
THE BOLT JERRY OF MAIN O/HANGING
... (FEP + 1 B&T Runner)

    Kenyo , Harlow .

STANWORTH

RALLY ~~E4 6c~~ E4/5 6b *Kenyo.*
    THE OLD A10 ROUTE RALEIGH
E3 6C *Rock head* ←frigger
ARMSTRONG E2 6a
    AN INDEPENDANT FINISH HAS BEEN
DONE UP THE WALL L OF APOLO, WITH
A RUNNER IN THAT ROUTE.

WILTON TWO

OR LIKE WELSH 5b!! Eh John! AG

THE HORNET   25FT E1 5B * * * * * * * * *.

(ALIAS:- PLEASE KEEP OFF THE GRASS ???)

CAN'T BE 5A - YOU CAN'T CLIMB THAT HARD...

CLIMB THE SMALL CORNER JUST LEFT OF THE BEE AND STEP
LEFT ABOVE THE GRASS LEDGE (WHICH IS OUT OF BOUNDS ???)
CLIMB THE WALL STRAIGHT UP.

SO, THE Hornet is only VS + (piz). + still shit!

This Route is ONLY
HUS 5a (if that). and
No Stars! Phil Kelly.
WILTON FOUR

JOHN HARTLEY (SOLO)   ? ? ?
22ND MARCH '84
almost as artificial
as cracked orange
(and don't forget it) PK

COLD EMOTION 30 FT E4 5C *

CLIMB THE RIGHT HAND SIDE OF THE STRIKING ARETE
RISING FROM THE PIT. (FRIDGE/FREEZER ZAWN ???)

good Route PK ??
(also did this twice John)

JOHN HARTLEY — (SOLO)
5TH APRIL '84
How many Times Did You Top Rope It First? Twice

LADY ICE 35 FT E4 6B * *

CLIMB THE LEFT HAND SIDE OF COLD EMOTION
ARETE. (1 PEG & 1 BOLT RUNNER)

THIS IS ON COLD EMOTION NOT LADY ICE. — NEVER HEARD OF BLINKERS!

why was the
bolt which mark
and I used on
the second ascent
chipped off John & did you not see it
on the first ascent!

JOHN HARTLEY
MARK HANK PASQUILL
14TH JUNE '84

SNAP

CRACK

POP

Tony Hennysyde

TUT! TUT! AG. (from Little Bowland Quarry)
Page 35

IT FELL OFF!
JUST LIKE YOU DID!

most Bits do if a crow bar is USED on THEM.

NO CROW BAR MATE
I JUST HIT IT WITH
A GYAKU ZUKE.
is that a sledge hammer PK

23

El Capitan

Wall of Early Morning light   (V.S ~~4b~~)   5A.
    Now free (all bolts chopped)
1 resting   point
  2 bivouacs

                         I Lonsdale
       25.9.81   P Clarke

La Escuela is not 5.11.

LONSDALE IS LYING AGAIN!

        We saw him using TWO

          resting points

                  A Hartnett
                  S Webster.

WILTON TWO

~~IRON ORCHID~~

IRON ORCHID E4 6~~B~~ ✝✝✝ 6a.

45ft. CLIMB DIRECT UP THE ARETE RIGHT OF
SWINE TO A PEG AT 25ft. MOVE RIGHT
ROUND THE CORNER INTO AN OVERHANGING
SCOOP. PEG RUNNER. CLIMB STRAIGHT UP
USING THE RIGHT EDGE OF THE SCOOP.

           JOHN HARTLEY.
           TONY PRESTON
           JIM BURTON

                2.4.82.

WILTON ONE   BLACK MAMBA NOW FREE. ✓
                         E4 6B.

SLING PRE PLACED ON HOOK BY AR,.
      Dougie Hall 25/4/82

5-5-82.

2nd Ascent   GRAVITY WELL (STANWORTH) E3/4 6B

(2nd 2.V.) Grade & Quality confirmed

Gaz Heneley (Sob:)!

19.4.82
ECGERTON QUARRY
* MALVINAS 50' MVS 4b
        - LEANING
    obvious corner 50' L of Cherry Bomb.
      1 MAKIN C FLETCHER

✦ ECGERTON QUARRY

I SHOT JASON KING   60ft E2 5b   FUCK A.T.
LEFT ARETE OF GALLOWS POLE WALL STARTING ON RIGHT
MOVE LEFT AT 15ft MOVE BACK RIGHT TO FINISH
                MICK JOHNSTON + IAN JOHNSTON
                    DONE SUMMER 1980.

WILTON ONE

EGO TRIP E5 6b **** (STET FREE).

John Monks
Tony Preston.
6/8/82.

WILTON FOUR.

E5 JM

STUDENTS SAUNTER E4 6c * (TEACHER'S CRACK FREE)

John Monks
John Hartley.
6/8/82

WILTON ONE

(50FT) SLEEPWALK E4 6A **** (FREE CLIMBS VACCINATION A1)

CLIMB THE SLAB JUST RIGHT OF ERYTHROCYTE TO A LEDGE MOVE
RIGHT AND CLIMB THE THIN CRACK TO A HORIZONTAL BREAK.
MOVE LEFT TO FINISH UP A GROOVE.

John Hartley
John Monks

6/8/82

WILTON ONE.

GRAVITATIONAL EXPERIMENT. E4 6C 50FT.   E35C PP.

CLIMB THE THIN CRACKS DIRECT UP THE WALL BETWEEN
JEAN AND CROWS NEST DIRECT.

John Hartley
John Monks
10/8/82.

2nd Ascent 16/8/82
E4 6b   harder for midgets!
0/10 for spelling
Poc B6b   [HE KNEW THE PP ETC BEFORE]
Mickey Mouse   [WE DID IT - HOWEVER!]
Of course!
P.B

HAIG   NOW FREE   6B

JOHN MONKS (SOLO)

12/8/82

"LANCASHIRE CRUMBLY"   LESTER MILL   (CHEESE BUTTRESS)

4' left of KLINK.   climb slab via scoop
direct to ledge   step right up finish up upper crack
of KLINK to ledge and then via arete.
45ft   Hard Severe 4a.   Dave Sanderson
                              Roger Bunyan

5/8/82

"THE OTHER MAN'S ALTERNATIVE"   LESTER MILL (SET BACK)

30' Just Severe. Climb crack 5' R. of 24B to
ledge. Traverse 10' R. Finish up short corner.

                              Dave Sanderson
              13/8/82   Roger Bunyan.

"HIT BY A LORRY"   45' Hard Severe 4a.   LESTER
                                          MILL
                                          (SET BACK)
20' from Neon Shuffle. Climb pedestal & wall to
ledge. Traverse 15' L. Climb loose corner to
finish.
                              R. Bunyan
              10/8/82   D. Sanderson.

"MOORLAND TOOTH HIGHWAY"   25' Hard Severe 4a.
                           LESTER MILL.   (SET BACK)

5' R. of 26. Climb crack R. of detached tooth to
ledge. Up corner to finish. Loose.
                              Roger Bunyan
                              Dave Sanderson.

              11/8/82.

'Cheese Buttress Area' LESTER MILL

"WHIP ME! WHIP ME!" Severe 20'.

Top of cone between 'Right Turn Groove' and 'Klink'.
Climb right crack to top, then up over blocks.
Top loose.

Roger Bunyan

Dave Sanderson.   5/9/82.

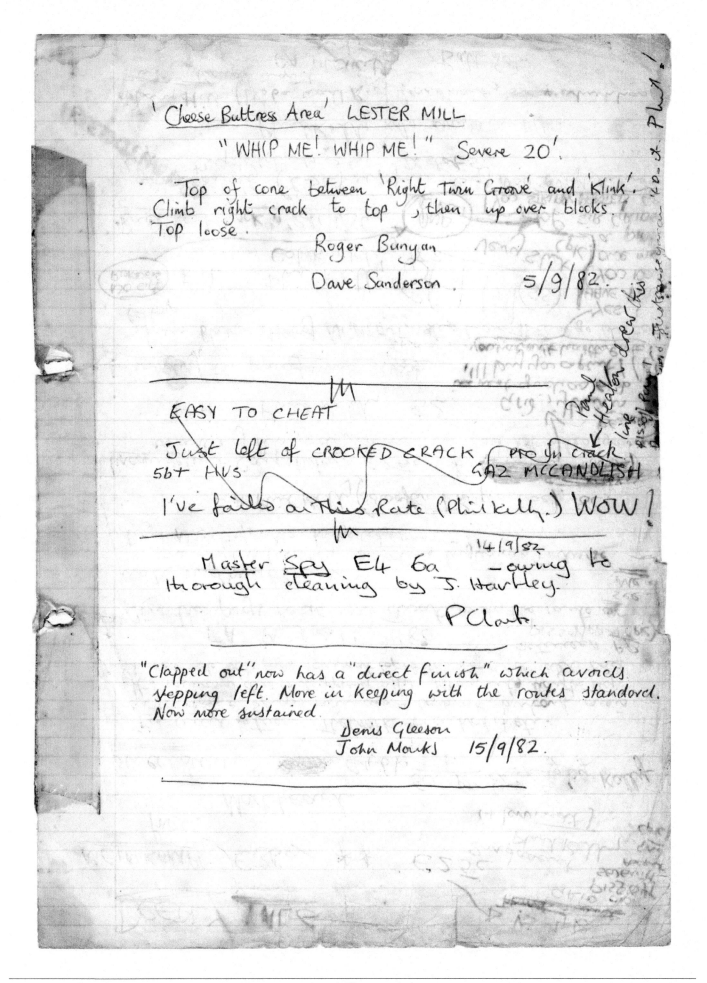

EASY TO CHEAT

Just left of CROOKED CRACK   pro in crack
5b+ HVS   GAZ McCANDLISH

I've failed on this Rate (Phil Kelly.) WOW!

Master Spy E4 6a   —owing to
thorough cleaning by J. Hartley.

P Clark.

"Clapped out" now has a "direct finish" which avoids
stepping left. Move in keeping with the routes standard.
Now more sustained.

Denis Gleeson
John Monks   15/9/82.

14/9/82

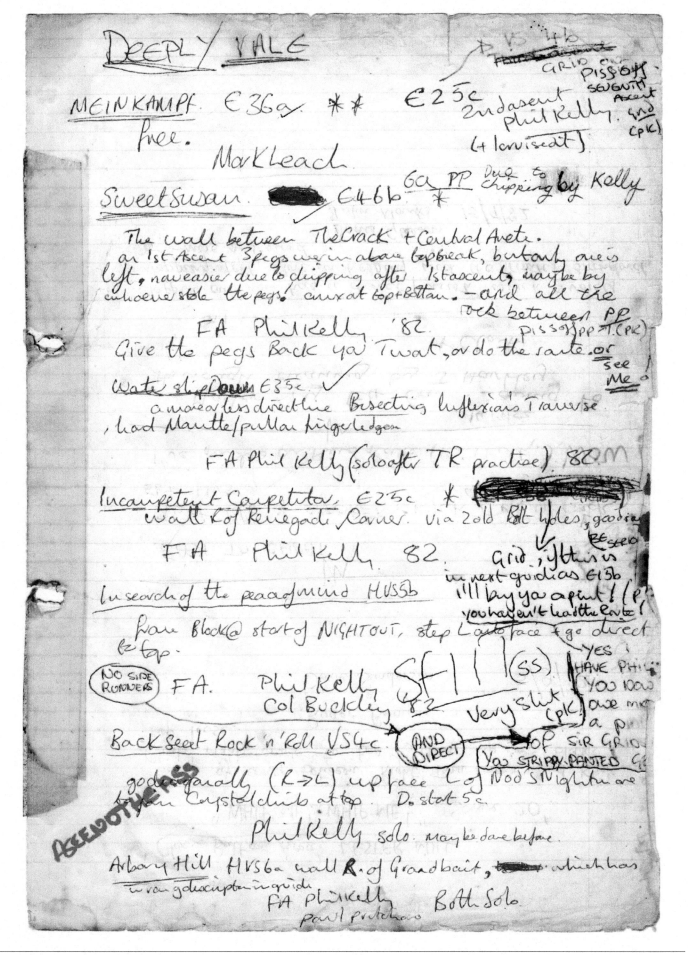

DEEPLY VALE

MEINKAMPF. E3 6a. ✱✱   E2 5c 2ndascent Phil Kelly. 2nd (PK)
free.   (+ 1onviscat)

Mark Leach.

Sweet Susan. ▬▬ E4 6b 6a PP Due to chipping by Kelly *

The wall between The Crack + Central Arete.
on 1st Ascent 3 pegs were in above top break, but only one is
left, now easier due to chipping after 1st ascents, maybe by
whoever stole the pegs! crux at top + bottom. – and all the
rock between PP
     FA Phil Kelly '82.   PISS Oyf PP → T. (PK)
Give the pegs Back yar Twat, or do the same. or
see
Me

Water slip Down E3 5c ✓
a more or less direct line Bisecting Inflexions Traverse
, hard Mantle/pullon tinger ledges

     FA Phil Kelly (solo after TR practise) 82 M

Incompetent Competitor E2 5c * ▬▬▬
wall L of Renegade Corner via 2 old Bolt holes, good sr

     FA Phil Kelly 82. Grid, if this is BE SERIO
in next guidias E1 5b
I'll buy ya a pint! (P)

In search of the peace of mind HVS 5b   you haven't lead the route!

from Block @ start of NIGHT OUT, step L and face + go direct
to top.

(NO SIDE RUNNERS) FA. Phil Kelly SF | | | (SS) YES
HAVE PHIL
Col Buckley 82   Very Slik (PK) YOU NOW
owe me
a p

Back Seat Rock 'n' Roll VS 4c (AND DIRECT) OF SIR GRID
You STRIPPY PANTED G

go diagonally (R→L) up face L of Nod's Nightmare
to join Crystal climb at top. D. start 5c

     Phil Kelly solo. maybe done before.

Arbory Hill HVS 6a wall R. of Grand bait, ▬▬ which has
in own god escription in guide.
FA Phil Kelly   Both Solo
paul pritchard

TRANGO TOWER
PILE OF BiZ
***

WEST FACE ROUTE, (NO NAME YET) 4,185' OF CLIMBING
16th June - 19th, 21st - 30th June inc retreat from face.
GRADE VI, 5.10B, A1, E6 (ITS REALY H.V.S 5A BUT
SERIOUS FOR THAT GRADE)

ALTHOUGH BY MODERN STANDARDS NOT A TECNICAL
DIFFICULT ROUTE, IT IS NEVER THE LESS A SERIOUS
UNDER TAKING. MAIN REASONS ARE, THE REMOTNESS OF THE
ROUTE, IE MORE THAN 15 MINS FROM MAIN ROAD. THE
WEATHER CAN PLAY A MAJOR PART, ABSEIL INSPECTION, PRE PLACED
RUNNERS, CLEANING, BRUSHING, CHIPPING HOLDS AND TOP ROPE
INSPECTION ALSO HARD TO ARRANGE.

START AT HEATHROW, CATCH THE 11.15AM to ~~ISLAMAB~~
ISLAMABAD, CHECK IN WITH MINISTRY OF TOURISM
(HAVING ALREADY BOOKED AND PRE PAID FOR PERMISSION
TO CLIMB ON THE KARAKORUM CLIMBING WALL) AND SPEND
5-6 days in RAWALPINDI AND ~~ISLAMABAD~~, ARRANGING
VARIOUS THINGS. THEN TWO DAYS DRIVE ON THE
KARAKORUM HIGHWAY TAKES YOU TO SKARDU. SPEND TWO
DAYS ~~HIRING~~ HIREING PORTERS AND TRANSPORT. DRIVE
TO DASSU (½ DAY) HIRE REST OF PORTERS TO CARRY
INSPECTION ROPES, CHIPPING DEVICES, WIRE BRUSHES
ect ESSENTIAL FOR MODERN DAY CLIMBING AND
THROW THEM IN THE RIVER INDUS. WALK 6-8
days to BASE CAMP. ANOTHER DAYS WALK TAKES
YOU TO THE FOOT OF THE ROUTE.

START 1000' to the ~~left~~ Right of the Original route.

1) 160' CLIMB STEEP SNOW UNTIL HANDS CAN GRASP
ROCK (DO NOT CHIP HOLDS YET). FOLLOW CRACK IN LEFT
WALL OF CORNER HARD MOVE OVER SMALL BULGE, MOVE
RIGHT TO GOOD STANCE, BELAY.

(2 150', STEP LEFT INTO CORNER CRACK SYSTEM, WIDE BRIDGING LEADS TO A SHALLOW GROOVE, FOLLOW THIS TO SHOULDER.

(3 160' EASY TRAVERSING (MURDER IN E.B.S) CROSS SNOW TO WALL ON LEFT.

(4 160' TRAVERSE DIAGONALLY LEFT CROSS STEEP SNOW TO (LIABLE TO SLIP OFF HERE IN E.B.S) ROCK ARETE. CLIMB THIS (POOR PROTECTION)

(5 155' GO DIAGONALLY LEFT UP SOFT SNOW, THEN MIXED GROUND TO BELAY ON LEFT OF LARGE CORNER, THIS IS A GOOD SITE FOR BIVI ON LEFT UNDER ROCK BULGE.

(6 160' TRAVERSE RIGHT TO CORNER, CLIMB THIS TO SMALL LEDGE BELAY ~~UNDER OVERHANG~~ ON SMALL LEDGE OVER BULGE. CARE SHOULD BE TAKEN ON THIS AND NEXT PITCH DUE TO LOOSE ROCK. (CANNOT BE CLEANED FROM ABOVE BEFORE HAND)

(7 160', CONTINUE UP CORNER TO BELAY BELOW LARGE ROOFS ~~&~~ MINISCULE STANCE.

(8 150', CLIMB UP FOR 20' TO JUST BELOW ROOFS, TRAVERSE RIGHT FOR 35' IN A VERY EXPOSED POSITION TO GAIN THE UPPER WALLS. GO BACK LEFT PEG BELAYS

(9 80', GO STRAIGHT UP LOOSE WALL ON LEFT OF SECOND (THEN YOU DON'T HIT HIM WITH LOOSE STONES) BELAY ON SLAB.

(10 110', UP STEEP SNOW TO MIXED GROUND (LOOSE) TO UPPER WALL. GOOD SITE FOR PORTER LEDGES (BECAUSE WE COULDN'T GO ANY FURTHER, IT WENT

31

(11 150', HAVE BREAKFAST, THEN TRAVERSE LEFT ~~FER~~ TO SLABS UP THESE TO JOIN ORIGINAL ROUTE.

(12 130' UP STEEP SNOW AND SLABS TO BELOW CORNER' ON LEFT. (3 LANES OF FIXED ROPE IN PLACE).

(13 140'. GAIN THE "SNOW PATCH" VIA CORNER AND GROOVE ABOVE (VERY TIREING JUMA CO'S ROPE FALLS LEFT UNDER ROOFS). BLOCK BELAYS.

(14 200', (SPLIT AT 50' WERE WE PITCHED A TENT) CLIMB ~~VEITHER~~ LEFT EDGE OF SNOWPATCH PEG BELAY IN SMALL ROCK BUTTRESS.

(15 100', TRAVERSE ~~RIGHT~~ WARE TO FOOT OF ~~THE~~ WALL, GOOD PORTER LEDGE SITE, AS WALL SHELTERS FROM ABOVE.(ONLY JUST)

(16 150', MOVE BACK LEFT AND UP TO SHALLOW CORNER UP THIS AND EXELLENT CRACKS ABOVE TO SMALL BELAY.

(17 140', GOOD CLIMBING LEADS UP CRACKS TO SEMI HANGING BELAY.

(18 140', ROOF'S NOW BLOCK THE WAY, AND IF ITS AROUND NOON YOUR BEING SHOWERED WITH ICICLES THE SIZE OF JAVALINES. CLIMB CRACK FOR 20' UNTIL IT DISAPPEARS, TENSION RIGHT FOR 40' (SEMI PENDULUM) THEN WHEN THAT DISAPPEARS EITHER PANIC AND FALL OFF OR HAVING ALREADY LEFT YOUR BRAINS WITH YOUR WALLET IN DASSU FRICTION LIKE MAD FOR A 50' HEADING FOR THE CORNER ONCE HERE HAVE A BREATHER AND MOVE RIGHT CLIMB STEEP WALL TO GOOD BELAY.

(19 160' - CLIMB CRACKS ABOVE KEEPING AN EYE ON

LOOSE FLAKES AT 80' TO BELOW OBVIOUS GROOVE.

(20 150' CLIMB WALL ABOVE TO GAIN GROOVE CLIMB LEFT WALL TO STANCE.

(21 100' UP THE WALL ABOVE AND THROUGH ROOFS VIA OBVIOUS BREAK, MOVE LEFT THEN BACK RIGHT TO BELAY

(22 120' THIS PITCH IS OVER LOOSE GROUND SO CARE SHOULD BE TAKEN NOT TO KILL YOUR SECOND; MOVE GINGERLY UP RIDGE ON RIGHT.

(23 80' SLIDE DOWN SNOW ON RIGHT TO A NOTCH, CLIMB THIS AND BELAY BELOW RIGHTWARD SLANTING CRACK

(24 160' EXCELLENT CLIMBING UP SLANTING CRACK LEADS INTO CORNER, UP THIS AND BELAY WELL BACK ON SLABS.

(25 160' STEP RIGHT AND CLIMB WALL TO OVERHANG, SWING LEFT AND UP TO BELOW A STRIKING OFF WIDTH CRACK CLIMB THIS (EXITING) TASEING ARM BARS, HEAD JAMS, ECT TO BELAY BEHIND A SMALL PINICAL.

(26 140' MOVE RIGHT AND CLIMB THE IMPRESSIVE HAND JAM CRACK TO SLOPING LEDGE. ABOVE IS AN ~~HORRENT~~ HORRENDOUS LOOKING OFF WIDTH CRACK, UP THIS WITH TREPIDATION UNTIL FEAR FORCES YOU RIGHT UP A THIN CRACK ~~TO~~ GOOD LEDGE.

(27 160' LAYBACK THE FLAKE ABOVE AND HAND ~~~~ TRAVERSE LEFT ~~~~ BACK INTO CRACK ~~~~ LINE HARD CLIMBING UNTIL ROPE RUNS OUT HANGING BELAY.

HOW SOON IS NOW. AVS 5a. 25'   Wilton 4.
Wall and between Gordons and Coke. No Belay
                    Stephen Hill (Solo, fell off Loather, burnt hands!).
                                        Ha Ha.

Parbold Main Quarry.   - Big quarry above Parbold Quarry
Prominent Nose Shaped Butress visible from Car Park.

The Nose.   HS.   35'
      Start 5' left of Nose, Climb to Grassy ledge, step Right and finish
up arrete.

Nose Direct   VS, 4C   35'.

      Start 5' Right of Nose, Climb direct to top half of the Nose

Desperation.   VS, 4C   35'.

      Groove in centre of Crag, goes through bushes, then climb straight up,
loose block half way   up.

        Above 3 routes   Stephen Hill, Paget Pugh.

Wilton 3 :-
        "Right Leg Eliminate" Loose Corner to
the left of Central Crack. Previously called
"Block and Tackle H'Diff" First ½ ascent by
Kevin Elliss :- No Second. Still awaits Second
ascent !

Shaggy Mamba   E5 6B.   XXX
excellent climbing. This route should have had
loads of ascents as it was put up 1½ years ago.
    2nd ascent

2 falls   get your
                                                 fingers out
                                                 Lads.

Run Wild Run Free (new name)
Black Pitch (Four Minute Miler) E6 6B XXX
This route has now had a second
ascent (or first ascent. No side runner
used in Ego Trip. Fantastic climbing.
Do not fall off first 20ft as most of
the nuts would probably strip.

1 fall
foot hold
snapped
Mark, How can you claim the first ascent of an established line, The true
first ascent was done by Phil Garlick esq. (one of Lancs. best climbers).
I think you're very, very silly, Mr Garlick esq. would not be very pleased.
                                                         Phil

    WILTON 1   (CHIMNEY BUTTRESS)

    CLEAN SWEEP   90' E5 6a   ***
    From the second peg on 'LOOPY'
    CRUCIFY the break leftwards past
    2 PR's. FINISH UP 'WAMBAT'.
        Paul Pritchard & Mark Leach.
    THE PITFACE.

    IS IT A CHEESECAKE OR A MERINGUE. 20' HVS 5a
    The   crack left of 'POWER OF THE MEKON'
        Paul Pritchard solo.

35

Wilton four.
Hells Bells   E5 6B
free climbs Bell Crack. 1 peg in sito.

(No falls).   Mark leach
              April 85

WILTON 1
BLACK DOG BLUES   50' E5 6B   *
Climb BLACK MAMBA to the P.R. and
lurch R.wards to the ledge and
PR on SHAGGY DOG, then take the
continuation crack above to finish in
the loose groove,
              Paul Pritchard e   16/5/85.
           ANDREW GRIDLEY

WILTON 1
MYRMIDON   50' E5 6B   ***
climb the left edge of 'OVERTAKERS
BUTTRESS' direct Post a very long
reach exiting the thin crack.
(MICRO WIRES ESSENTIAL)

This route FA - Paul Pritchard
is easy for the
Tall and   belayed by A GRIDS
Possibly   seconded by PHIL KELLY. (well almost)
impossible for
the short. PP
       'SECOND ASCENT   E4 6B
            M. Leach
              M. LEACH   ***
                       SORRY ABOUT THE
                       RIGGIN!

1	MIXED VEG		H.V.S.	5b
1A	MIXED VEG DIRECT START		H.V.S.	5b
2	EUIh CRYSTAL		E1	5b
3	THE BEAST		E3	5c/6A
4	RSCHARGHADO		E3	5c
5	NONSTOP SCREAMER		E3	5b
6	RETURN TO FANTASY		E2	5b/c
7	DOOMS DAY		VS	4c

EGERTON

THE ~~RHYTHM~~ OF THE HEAT   E1 5C   35'

On the end of the red prow there is
a diagonal crack from R to L, climb
up easy rock to this and go direct
up the wall ~~½ away~~ where the ck goes left

KNAT ATTACK   VS 4C   40'
Start as for Rhythm and traverse
R at the break to a flared
hanging crack, climb this to a
sloping finish.
DONE DIRECT LIKE IT SHOULD   a crap route
HAVE BEEN DONE AT FIRST BY A SUPERSTAR anyway
suicidal. ~~The Lamb Lies Down EA b~~
                                              E4 6a
THE LAMB LIES DOWN ON BROADWAY
                                              60' (
The arête left of NEIGHBOURHOOD
Threat, (PR & Pro in this route).
Start on left & move right
½ maybe to big ledge, either belay or go L onto Arête + to top.'
ALL BO Paul Pritchard
        Phil ~~( )~~ ~~Guy~~ KELLY

WILTON 1 (white wall)
                                              E4 6a
~~THE GOOSE OF PARADISE OF LIFELESS~~
CRATER TRAITOR E4 6a ~~PACKED 60'~~

The vague groove line left of
Dandelion groove. climb direct
to the in situ RURP and traverse
R to two vertical Pods Finish
direct. Definately worth doing. Serious   (This phrase has)
                                          (nothing to do)
Ja Paul Pritchard   (with his phisique)
    Steve 'Tarzan' SHARPLES

Can someone Do it DIRECT?
The DIRECT has now gone with 1PR. E5 6a
very serious   (sorry it wasn't)
        Paul Pritchard 2nd Ascent   (I did the 2nd pp.)
        Gaz McCANDLISH   P.K + new five's + yellow tights.

WILTON ONE   PITFACE

THE DEATH OF TIMOTHY GRASS * HVS   5a (I THINK).

LIES BETWEEN "THE" and "ERYTHROCYTE".
CLIMB ~~LEFT~~ ~~OF~~ THE LEFT HAND CRACK,
AT FIRST LEDGE STEP OUT LEFT ONTO
WALL AND CLIMB DIRECT TO TOP OVER
THE ~~~~ OVERHANGING BULGE.

GRIDS , STEVE (TARZAN) SHARPLES

NOTE WITH A BIT OF CLEANING
THIS COULD BE A CLASIC (TONGUE IN
Go Trundle it Grid! CHEEK)

WILTON 3

THE GAY DWARFS AND Mr PLOD GO TO
THE TUPERWARE PARTY.   E2   5b   45'

CLIMB the bulging wall right of
crooked crack moving left at the
top (No side runners (like Grid used). A bit
loose and not really worth doing
unless you've done all the others.

   Paul Pritchard - sight solo.

how can you sight solo something you took
2 days to clean?
     (PK)

DONE MONTHS
AGO BY MICK LOVAT } TRUE ON
& JOHN HARTLEY } SIGHT
     SOLOS.

THE SCREAM OF THE BUTTERFLY   E3 5b/c

The wall between crater traitor and Dandelion groove Terminating in twin cracks and a right facing scoop. NECKY (it makes use of tied ~~off Friends~~). adequate holds and excellent pro. you soft lump of shit.
        Gaz MECANDERISH.
        Paul Pritchard —

who said Gaz was a/man? AP/

E2 5b
(PK)

DONE   LAST YEAR — CALLED
'RED FLOWERS ARE RED'
AND   E1 — (Not at all serious for men !)
        Dai Lampard
        Nig. Holmes.
        Rupert Bear

SEE P. 62

you tell the young upstarts Dai !

what Did I tell you Gary ? (Phil)

I Said "RED FLOWERS ARE RED" you said "Scream of the Butterfly"
Then I said look at the Dog's Book,
Then you said "PISS OFF"
Now you'll say "Shit ,!
Phil a pint !"

VETERAN ~~~~ COSMIC ROCKER   E3 5C   (3" HIGH   sit and swivel Gridley   NOT WORTH PISSING ON 4J)
The arête ~~~~ right of Flytrap. start below the triangular roof, swing left and climb the arête on its left. (Quite artificial but good moves) Can anyone climbs the arête on its right as this would be much better and much harder. YES MARK LEACH CAN AND DID.

E2 5b
Phil Kelly   Paul Pritchard   both led;
        Gaz mcanderlish   no, I climbed Flytrap actually
3rd Ascent. (maybe you used holds in Flytrap)

Page 35 GRID'S BOLT PAGE! (MOSTLY ONE BIG LIMESTONE ROOF!)

LITTLE BOWLAND Quarry

(BET YOU CANOT FIND IT).

iX us.

1. VISIONS OF CHINA (E1 5B) SOLO STEVE SHARPLES. *
TAKES THE OVERHANGING WALL NEXT TO THE ROOF UP A DIAGEONAL

2. BATTLE OF — THE BULGE (HVS 5A). GRIDS. SOLO **
TAKES THE BULGE RIGHT OFF THE ABOVE WALL

3. SPACE WALK E3 6b AP E56b RF. (E1 5C) GRIDS SOLO *
AS FOR ① BUT! HAND TRAVERSE ACROSS EDGE OF OVERHANG 10 FEET TO A BUTTRESS ABOVE THEN EITHER DROP OFF OR PULL UP ONTO THIS BUTTRESS STRAIGHT TO TOP A LITTLE PUMPY.

4. SONS OF PIONEERS. (HVS 5R)
S. SHARPLES SOLO
FROM BETWEEN ① AND ② a crack starts at about 15 FEET AND TERMINATES A FANONY. CLIMB THCS

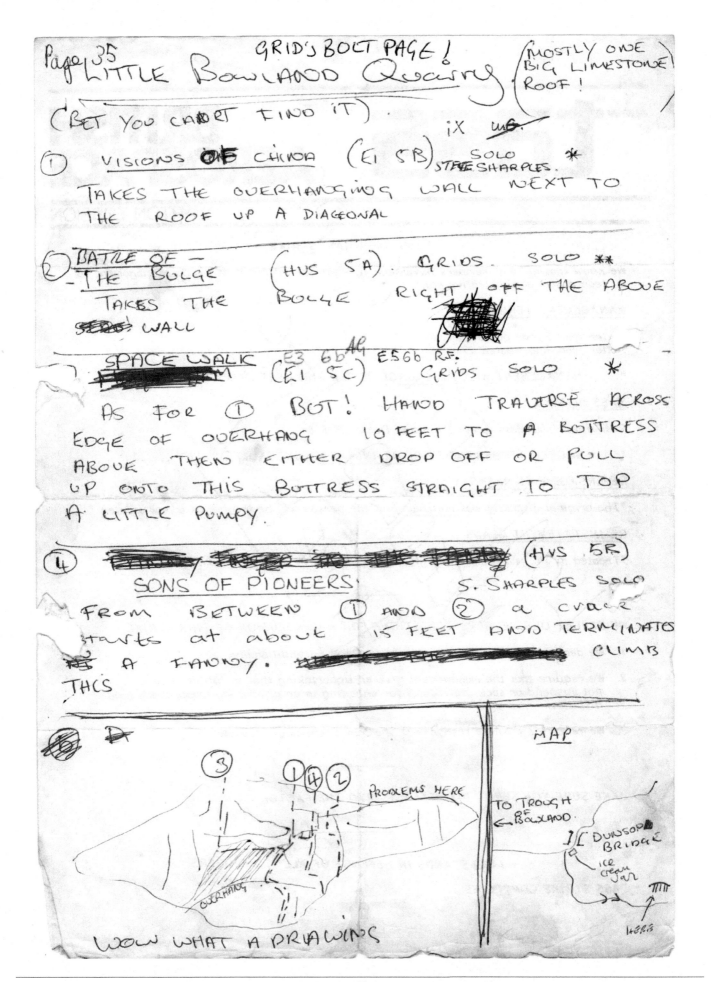

MAP

PROBLEMS HERE

TO TROUGH BF BOWLAND.

DUNSOP BRIDGE
ICE CREAM JAR

HERE

OVERHANG

WOW WHAT A PRIAWING

WILTON 1

THE THIN WHITE LINE 35FT E3 6A ★★

CLIMBS THE OBVIOUS THIN CRACK TO
THE RIGHT OF WHITE SLABS BUNT TO THE BELAY LEDGE.
FINISH AS FOR WHITE SLABS BUNT

TIM LOWE
BERNIE BRADBURY 16.8.84
~~Maybe~~ E4 (pk)
Definitely E4 6a.

CHANCE ENCOUNTER 30FT E3 5C ★★

CLIMBS THE DIAMOND SHAPED BUTTRESS
TO THE LEFT OF UNDERTAKERS CRACK. PEG RUNNER
AT 25 FEET.

TIM LOWE
DAVE JOSE
DEREK KENYON 16.8.84

VETERAN COSMIC ROCKER   E3 6B   25'

THE same as the old route but laybacked on the right above the roof.

It 25' HVS 5,6 (more like E2/pk)
The wall left of this.

both the solo efforts
of mr Mark Leach esq
Don Roler

The prayer battery E3 5c   Ousell's Nest Quarry

The route takes the obvious pod groove around 20ft right of No 12 (Angel Delight) climb the pod and finish up the blocky crack (crux). One of the few routes at the Quarry with a good finish not needing a machette ~~on top of the quarry~~ at the top good tree belay at top. This is a good route and anyone who says "bag of choss" is fooling themselves. So no comments till you've done it please.

Led by G. Hibbert.
Seconded M. Bradshaw.

8, 8, 84

Sorry wrong route

Hawks Hill Quarry

The Golden Moment E4 6a ★ ★ ★

From 1st flatholds 10' up Bastille Day (q.v.) traverse L. past a peg Runner. to large sloping hold, bar here, go up the thin CK (crux) to a fingerhold; then go L. to the arete + climb this on its R.H. side to finish

Best
Route
@ Hawks

FA Phil Kelly,
Dave Whittles. July 84

~~WOOLLY + PASTA RACE~~ XS 6b.
THE ATOMIC ROOSTER
climbs the hanging flakes + hanging Sentry Box 10' R of Bastille Day, exiting left at the top. loose

← phil
you're just so good.

FA Phil Kelly unseconded
Nigel Booth held Ropes.

July '84.

After 3∞ Toprope Practices (OVER 18 MONTHS!)

44

Howclus Hill Qy Cwtt.

Bronze Medal, HoS-46

climbs the L. arete of Bastille Day Buttress

on its right hand side. Very Crap

Phil Kelly S/o. July 84.

S. Bancroft 1973

NOTE ON PARADOX! WHILTON 1

PARADOX HAS FALLEN DOWN AT ABOUT
15 ft. LEAVING LOOSE BLOCKS. THESE
HAVE NOW BEEN REMOVED BY
WAY OUT CLEANING TECHNIQUES BUT
THERES STILL A LOOSE 6 HUNDRED
WEIGHT BLOCK SO CARE MUST
BE TAKEN FOR THE FIRST 30 FEET

A. GRIDS!

N.B.
CONTRARY TO
POPULAR BELIEF
John Hartly HAD WITH
nothing TO DO AN
THIS TWAS AN
EARTHQUAKE

— THATS WHAT YOU
THINK
J.H.

BOLT IT John
BOLT IT

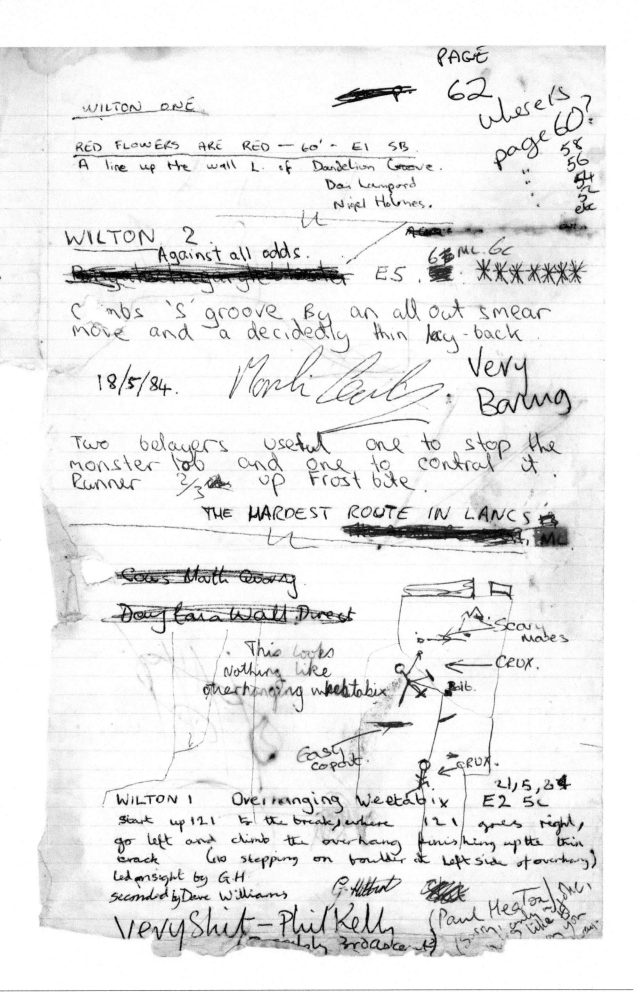

WILTON ONE

RED FLOWERS ARE RED — 60' — E1 5B.
A line up the wall L. of Dandelion Groove.
　　　　　　　　　　Dan Lampard
　　　　　　　　　　Nigel Holmes.

WILTON 2.
　　　Against all odds.
~~Red golden jungle route~~　　E5.　6a ML. 6c ✳✳✳✳✳✳

C'mbs 'S' groove By an all out smear
move and a decidedly thin lay-back.

18/5/84.　　Monk Cowl.　　Very Boring

Two belayers useful one to stop the
monster lob and one to control it.
Runner ⅔ up Frost bite.

　　　　THE HARDEST ROUTE IN LANCS.　ML

~~Cows Mouth Groovy~~.

~~Douglara Wall Direct~~

• This looks
Nothing Like
overhanging weetabix
　　　　　　　　　　　　　Scary
　　　　　　　　　　　　　Mares
　　　　　　　　　　CRUX.
　　　　　　　　Bolt.
Easy
copout.
　　　　　　　　CRUX.
　　　　　　　　　　21,5,84

WILTON 1　Overhanging Weetabix　E2 5c
Start up 121 to the break, where 121 goes right,
go left and climb the overhang finishing up the thin
crack　(no stepping on boulder at left side of overhang)
Led onsight by G.H
Seconded by Dave Williams　　G. Hilbert
Very Shit – Phil Kelly　　(Paul Heaton)
possibly 3rd ascent

WILTON 1 (PROW)

PATHETIQUE   E5 6a/b   *
Start midway between Camio &
wedgwood and climb direct to the
ledge (step L to arrange Pro in Camio).
climb the rugositied wall on the
right with fear and finish up
the pleasant thin crack in the upper wall
L of the finish of christeena.
     Fa Paul Pritchard
          Dave Peace.

Anglezarke
     Dancing on the Valentine.   E2 5c.   50ft.
Start up Mutamorphosis to the first ledge
+ climb the wall above just L of the arete.
                    15/2/85
                         M hiptrot.

Agrajag   E3 6a.   (direct start to G.T.)
     Up the thin crack R. of Golden Tower start,
to overlap. Move L (runner in G.T). Step back
R and go up centre of wall.
                    15/2/85
                         M hiptrot.

47

Dear Ian,

Please could you put the following in the new routes book. (off to France this week so time to call in).

Troy Quarry (N. Face). 20ft right of Anxiety, 4ft left of arête

"What I'd give for a Friend" H.V.S. 5a. 45ft.
Climb to V. shaped slot and follow steep cracks above. 13.7.85. F.A. Alan Cameron
John Mason

Thanks a lot, it was very dirty, with loose rock and sods, and didn't appear to have been done though obvious and good.

Hope the leg is getting better and you'll soon be burning up the rock.

All the best
John Mason.

48

19/7/84.

ANGLEZARKG Q7.

20ft.

THE FROGS HAVE LANDED. 5c.

The Wall L. of Nightmare.

Paul Heaton.

Write your witty remarks here: →

I was absolutely bamboozled
- Andy Hall xx

a boring Problem, Dave Before
eg 1982 Phil Kelly. [Fillsbrill]

Phil you're so cool

WILTON 2

IM CURED BOUNCY BOUNCY

maybe HVS E1 ~~5~~ 6a 1g
GRIDS
BUT BOMB OFF
you chukar!
no runners

STARTS JUST LEFT OF THE
GRASSY CORNER NEXT TO THE
MUD (35) CLIMB DIRECT UP
THE FACE TO THE BULGE
THEN LAYAWAY WITH SMEARS
UP THE SCOOP TO THE TOP

A. GRIDS (SECOND DID NOT
FOLLOW FELL
ASLEEP WITH BORDOM)

GOOD ROUTE
DESERVES
MINUS STARS

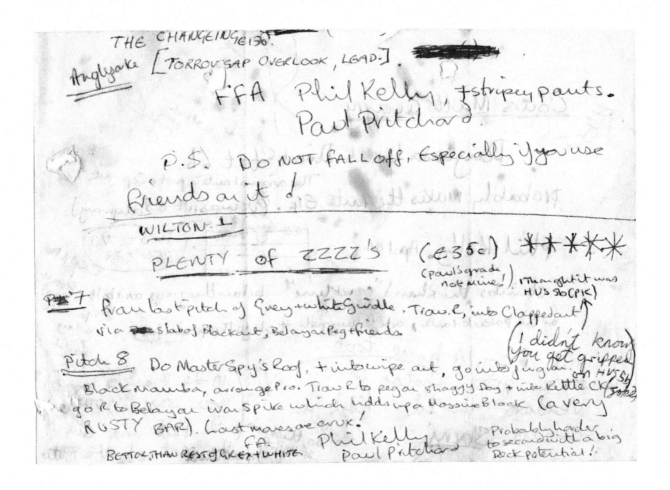

THE CHANGEING (E1b).

Anglyzake [TORROU SAP OVERLOOK, LGAD.].

FFA. Phil Kelly, + stripey pants.
Paul Pritchard.

P.S. DO NOT FALL OFF, Especially if you use
friends on it!

WILTON: 1

PLENTY of ZZZZ's   (E3 5c)   ✳✳✳✳✳

(paul's grade
not mine!) I thought it was
HUS 5b (PK)

P*7 From last pitch of Grey + white Girdle. Trav. L, into Clappedout
via slab of Blackout, Belay on Peg + friends.

(I didn't know
you get gripped
on HVS!)

Pitch 8   Do Master Spy's Roof, + into wipe out, go into jugbar
Black mamba, arrange pro. Trav R to regain shaggy Dog + into Kettle CK (some)
go R to Belay on war spike which hidds up a Massive Block (a very
RUSTY BAR). Last moves are crux!

F.A.   Phil Kelly
BETTOR THAN REST of GREX + WHITE   Paul Pritchard

Probably harder
to second with a big
Dock potential!

Cows Matti Quarry

Deytara Wall Direct Start 6b.

The original route is just a Cop-out.
probably makes the route E4. (It wasn't E5 anyway).

phil Kelly. April '84.

climbs the Rhand "cicktine" below the jugs and bolt, PAUL
on the parent route, at sluggish + slightly painful,

and I could have took
some good photo's in
Verdon if I'd had a
camera. Sorry.

(In the Blacks book
you say you'd it Phil and did
the rest of the route

wot NO
BELAYER

CRAM

a bloody good problem
pk

WILTON ONE

20ft   NO YOUR QUITE RIGHT ITS A
                    CHEESECAKE   HVS 5c

ANOTHER GREAT CLASSIC FROM THE LONGRIDGE
GANG. THE LEFT ~~EDGE~~ SIDE OF THE SLIM BUTTRESS
RIGHT OF CHRISTMAS CHIMNEY. (STAY WELL AWAY FROM
       A. GRIDS   CRACK
          J. MARSDEN   THE GROTTY ~~PIT~~)

WILTON ONE

20ft   COME ON YEE REDS.   VS 4b

LEFT ARÊTE OF CHRISTMAS CHIMNEY   303⁄4½

        ~~A GRIDS~~ ~~SOLO~~ IAN MAKIN when he was
                              about 30 years old.

(SECOND ASCENT) : I ~~THOUGH~~ I WAS
        BLINKY ~~to~~ POOR PAW Jams
〰〰〰〰〰〰〰〰〰〰〰〰〰〰

WILTON 2   WHAT A BAG OF CHOSS A GRIDS
                  AND I KNOW ABOUT CHOSS
       RAPID
I'M THE ~~GAY~~ RAMBLER, FONDLE FONDLE VS 4c ☠
The obvious loose/grassy groove left of "the Nod"
Brilliant climbing in an exposed situation!
   FA. P.KELLY
      P.PRITCHARD   31st May '85.
〰〰〰〰〰〰〰〰〰〰〰〰〰

JOSEPH HOLT (FORMERLY WHITE HORSE)

NOW FREE E5 6C
J. MONKS (SOLO)
18.7.83

"PINNACLE PROBLEM"

Lester Mill Quarry. Start as for
Left Twin Groove. 15' up, climb left
crack of the pinnacle. Stand on
pinnacle and then climb the two walls
above.
40' Severe.
Nigel Bunyan & Roger Bunyan.
(24.7.83)

ANGLEZARKE

"MISSION IMPOSSIBLE"   70'   **E2** 5b

Climb Terra Cotta (73) to the break below
the roof. Traverse this leftwards past a
horrendous block to First Finale (76) then
pull up L and finish as for Zarke (77). Can
be used as a harder first pitch to High Rewer
(74). Good.
Mark Liptrot + John Dodd
(31 July 83).

"ELAINE"   HVS   6a

The wall just left of Wedge (93) (avoiding the)
(square cut hold on the right) Take the
good thin crack above the break. A good
little problem.
Mark Liptrot (Solo)
(31 July 83)

↖ (*)
Should be at
Brownstones, but
left all those out
as well

WILTON 1

JOIN THE ARMY GET YOURSELF KILLED   E4 6b   * *

The arete. left SOIXANTE NEUF climbed direct from the
ground clip a peg (good) and finish on the
left of the rib

FA   Roland Foster NZ
Belayed CHRIS HARDY

SHAGGY MAMBA   E6 6b   * * *

Climbs Black Mamba clips the bolt and then climbs
direct up to the jug on Shaggy Dog without using
groove for holds or runners.
The best route at Wilton

FA   Roland Foster   NZ
Belayed Chris Hardy

REGRADINGS IN WILTON 1

GRAVITATIONAL EXPERIMENT   E3 6a
SILENTLY SCREAMING   E3 5c
THE DEVILS ALTERNATIVE   E3 6b
ASTRADYNE   E5 6a
SLEEP WALK   E3 6b
VAMPIRE   E3 5c

All done by Roland Foster

Troy Quarry.
6A. Direct start to One Step Further
Wilton One. path leads

DONE YEARS AGO BY - (Paradox Direct Finish 5A)
GEOFF MANN + DOUG SHAW   path leads.

Haghban.

New Wave 3rd Ascent good route (E3 6B)
Mark Leach Wonder whats all the
chalk plastered on for

Hello Phil
From Griff
23/9/18

(Cos PHIL KELLY MHA) A
ROPE EPIC

SCROUNGING
(IT)

Watch yourself sonny

G'day digger

HOGHTON QUARRY

ALL ROADS (LEAD) TO ROME.   E3 6b 2d Ascent Roland Foster ***

ES ~~6c~~ ***   1301.

A superb technical route right of Boudicea. Gain the Sinuous Crack from the left and follow it, sustained and technical, past I.P.R. and situ ~~wire~~ to the sandy break of "LEVEE". Pull straight up the bald wall above it make at technical "rock over" to a P.R. Continue direct past this by a desperate "No hands friction up". From the grassy ledge move left to finish up Boudicea.

F.A. GARY GIBSON, ADAM HUDSON 30/6/83.

Wilton 1

POWER OF THE MEKON   E1 5c *   30'

Climbs the wall left of "REGGATTA DE BLANC" Start below two small pockets and climb the wall direct.

I failed on this too — Phil Kelly

2b Ron Fawcett   F.A.   Daniel Williams.
  4c   Paul Heaton.

~~5b~~   boulder   problem   G.H.   solo FUCK OFF GEOFF.
5b H.U5 (nice move) Ian L.   → P.H.
  3a Paul Heaton   FUCK OFF TWICE (GEOFF.)
~~DENHAM~~   GEOFF (NAE ROPE) HIBBERT GEOFF!
                SHOW US YOUR NUTS.

THIS IS SURELY LARGER THAN ACTUAL SIZE + Bigger than the Route!

The Screaming Mee-Mees.   E3 6a

Takes the Roof and groove left of the Superciliousness — finish on the right:

R. Foster, G. Rimmer, M. Harbun, M. Lyon.
~~TROY QUARRY~~ (Harbingdon)

~~FRAZER~~   HVS 5a

The right hand of 2 obvious grooves between PIKE and CAPTAIN MAINWARING

P. Cain G. Rimmer

I did not write this —
Paul Heaton

DONE YEARS AGO R. HINDLE.

<u>TROY QUARRY</u>

DADS ARMY   HVS 4c   corner
The painfully obvious indepedent right of C. Mourering
which has a roof at half height. Finish up the groove
above
                    G Rimmer P CAIN

<u>HOGHTON</u>

New Wave   2nd Ascent - R. Fother (N2) upgraded to
            E4 6c?

<u>YORKSHIRE</u>   ?? Sorry Ian

Alternative Scar

Apex Buttress
<u>No Sexual Athletes Please.</u> E2 6a
The obvious nail between Red Light and Negative Groove.
Start up the crack move left then back right to a
junction with Red Light. Direct over the bulge to the
top.

NON OF THOSE ARE   → G Rimmer M Ryan D PEACE
SEXUAL ATHLETES - RUMOR   ↑
                                        WELL, HE TOUCHED
                                        THE HOLDS.
    LCHOVER GROOVE DIRECT START   HVS 5c
↗ The direct start, probably done before, but not
recorded

BRILLIANT ROUTE. FOR G Rimmer / Solo
Male Hoedown ~~~~ YORKSHIRE.

~~Jimmy Nip~~ NIP WILTON ONE

    JIMMY NIP. NOW FREE E4 6b? (RAINING)   E3 6a

        J. MONKS.
        ROPES HELD BY MICK BLOOD.

WILTON 1

FALLING WALL   E1   5b   45'

20' L of Willow Arete. Climb the thin crack to the small ledge, then the wall above.

Tim Low
Dave Vose   19.5.83

ANGLEBARKE

TURKISH DELIGHT   VS. 5b.   60'

Parallel line of flakes just L of Kebabs with hard start. From Big ledge traverse L and finish up Elder Grove,

Mark Liptrot (Solo)
8.6.83.

Names of Superb and Grand transposed in new guide. ML/DT.

ELAINE   HVS   6a.   30'

Boulder problem wall, just left of Wedge (avoiding square-cut 'hold on the' right). From break finish up good thin crack on L.   30/7/83
Mark Liptrot. (solo).

VISHNU (direct start)   E1 5c
The thin crack 10' R of the original start.
31/7/83
M. Liptrot. (solo).

MISSION IMPOSSIBLE   70' E2. 5b
Up Terra Cotta to break below roof. Traverse this L to First Finale, pull up left + finish as for Zorke. A good pitch, can be used as an alternative (harder) 1st pitch to High Revver.

M. Liptrot / John Dodd

30/7/83

HOGHTON QUARRY

"LAMENTABLY GENTLEMANLY"   E5 6b   90ft
    ↳ never 6c more like 6a — 5b.

Supercedes "Spider Ride" by elementing pointless belay and
adding direct finish.
    Climb thin crack ~~~~ with three pegs up to the roof, move
left for 6 ft to below corner on top wall, climb through roof
and up corner (scary).

                FA Roland Foster   7-8-83
                    John Noblett

GETTING RID OF THE ALBATROSS   E6 6c   ***   90ft

Climbs the wall 10 ft left of "Lamentably Gentlemanly"
Up leftwards curving crack to niche, move right o-move and
the up to small roof move left (3 PR's) oh! and then power
up the top wall via the thin crack.

                FA Roland Foster   14-8-83

FOR GOD'S SAKE, BURN IT DOWN!   E3 6b   ***   120 ft.
        Takes the crack between Boadicea and Every Face
Tells a Story to join the latter above a small rhaddy.
Follow E.F.T.A.S. free to the break, move R and
zip up the finger crack to join the last few moves
of Boadicea.
                FA Male Haslam   9/8/83.
                    Greg Rimmer

a really good
route 2nd
ascent R7

N.B. EVERY FACE is still worth doing with its P.A.

GOLDEN DELICIOUS   E2/3 5c   ***
                        7/8/83
① Climb ~~~~ Gleb Ne.v 2 hin to belay ledge.

② At the edge of the belay ledge climb crack
to the roof (2PR). Turn left to the edge of
the small ledge clip PR on long sling and
swing ~~~~~~~ to the end of the Mandarin traverse.
Move up then left ~~~ jugs around the arête
to jugs and finish up crack trending right
to tree belay on Mandarin
        FA Dave Cronshaw
            Mick RYAN (using heist etim)

HOGHTON

"THE BURNING DESIRE"   E5 6b   90 ft.

GATH - Now completely free and absolutely superb

        FFA   D Kenyon (with rests)

           aluminised by R Foster (15/8/83)

→ . Leicester Mills (Evil wall)
"NONE STOP SCREAMER"
~~"Bath Side"~~   E3 5b   75' **

Start 15' Right of "Rorper".

Climb blocks & thin crack to obvious black
groove. Follow this to sloping ledge on
left & finish up short wall. Good belay an
ledge.   Dave Cronshaw, David Etherington, John Ryden
                    23.8.83

STANWORTH

a traverse of Apollo wall

"Voyager   "   XS 5c   *

Start up 'Jovi' & follow obvious
horizontal break to finish up
christ I can't remember what the last route is
but I'll go & get guide (Gemini.)
          Dve Cronshaw on himself
                28 4 83

WILTON 3   70ft

***   FIRE AND THEFT   E2/3 5c

THIS NOW ELIMINATES THE NEED FOR A TYROLEAN ON THE
BETTER THAN IT LOOKS!   THIRD PARTY
    BIG SWING POTENTIAL

STARTS FROM MID WAY UP THE '40 FOOT
CORNER ROUTE LEFT OF CANINE CRUX.
    SECOND SWAYS AROUND THE
ARETE AND BELAYS ON THE
CRUX OF CANINE. LEADER
THEN FOLLOWS THROUGH AND
TRAVERSES RIGHT UNDER THE
OVERLAP TO BRASTIUM REVERSE
BRASTIUM 3ft AND SWAY ACROSS
BETFIS WALL (P.R.) AND ACROSS
TO ROUTE TWO (CRUX)

        F.A. A. GRIDS
            S. SHARPLES

Wilton 3

        ASCENDVEASS   E1 4b

    Up the recently opened
crevice Pull of Poo
(THE REMAINS OF ~~SINISTER~~ DEEP CRACK & CHOCKSTONE CRACK)
A little runny   A Death route
                    I thought I was doesn't
FA A. GRIDS   dead and I   on the route!
    P. KELLY   J.H.
    G.... M...

STAR PAGE!
FOR REAL
MEN
****

BROWN-STONES QY
DC-10 15' E5 2b -5C (DEPENDING ON WE'NT)

THE ULTIMATE VARIENT ON THE MAGIC
THE ART OF DYNOING INTO THE 3RD DIME. INVOLVING
TOTAL FREE FLIGHT (ONLY FOR THE MENTALY UNSTABLE AE.)

EXTENDING

PHSYCIC
STANCE

EQUIPMENT:
BAKERS HAT
CHIN GUARD
GUM SHEILD
VERY STICKY BOOTS
3LbS O' DOPE
FULL CHALK BAG (BIG ENOUGH
TO PUT YOUR
BRAIN IN)

DANGER
AN OVERSHOOT
FROM THE
3 TRAJECTORY
SHOWN WOULD
END IN TERMINAL
INJURY

TG'S BLOOD STAIN
CRUX
CRASH LANDING
ON SLAB
KNEE
PADS
CONTROLED
DECENT
(OPTIONAL
SECOND PITCH)
CIAL
FOOTHOLD

KITE
VARIENT
(E2 1b)
FOR WIMPS

FIRST FREE DESCENT Pa. Pithard eag
(BASE JUMPER EXTRAORDINARE)
SECOND DESCENT
TIM GRIDLEY
A GOB SMACKING
ROUTE

Dear Ian,
	Just a short note with a new route that I did at
Anglezarke the other day.I did intend to drop in and write in the
new route book myself but got way-layed.Hence my reasons for sending it
via you to the new route book.Hope thats OK.Anyway the info:-

ANGLEZARKE

Septic Think Tank   70ft E5,6a   ***
As good a route as any on the wall left of Golden Tower offering
typically excellnt wall climbing with a bold feel and some very long
reaches.It takes the wall right of Please Lock Me Away.Start as that.
1)70ft.Follow the flake of that route to the break of Lucky Strike.
Move right along this to a peg runner,then lurch straight up the
wall for distant holds.Continue direct with an alarming stretch for
a ledge and peg runner,then more easier(5c) climbing direct up the now
less spooky wall.

First ascent:Gary Gibson,unseconded (Hazel Gibson held rope) 13/5/'98

	Any other info you get in I would be glad of for the magazine.
I am alos interested in printing a new route up-date in the mag to
Lancashire at the end of the year;interested in helping?

				All the best

					Paul

Anglezarke Qy   Toad route, -VS 5b.
                                         20'

Does this grade exist-?

Wall between 101 + 102

A bold new concept of the modern idiom
epitomizing bouldering at its best.
Quality of climb was quickly realised,
with 2 repeat ascents within 10 seconds.   (3 years)
(Reported to be hard in nails)
On sight solo - Andy Hay.
2nd ascent

"its a little shit! I thought I was smelly, phew!" Andy Kay

I have done this route - Paul Heaton.

So what? - Paul Heaton   Shut up Paul! Andy xxx

Strong language eh?

ANGLEZARKE   (HVS 5a) Paul ? Did you tear this out
                                          All my love Sandra.

64

WILTON TWO.

XXX PIGS ON THE WING DIRECT FINISH.
(Totalleg supercedes) the original route
by climbing the wall left of the
thin crack above the ~~bra~~ bucket.
Immaculate climbing at E6 6B.

Led by ~~Phils Clurch~~ 1st ascent

also led by ~~Paul~~ Pritchard 2nd ascent.

3rd April in the year of ~~our~~ Lord
1985 A.D. (A fine day was had by
all.)
↑ IS THIS DOG — HANGDOG,
DAY, JOHN, DAY! OR BLACKDOG?

BOLDLY GOES WHERE JOHN HARTLEY DIDN'T

PP

> HOW CAN THIS BE WHEN YOU HAVE TO CLIMB
> HALF (THE BETTER HALF) OF PIGS ⊕ TO GET
> TO YOUR VARIATION FINISH.

> AT LEAST I DIDN'T ~~TOP ROPE~~
> IT OR GET SOMEONE TO CHALK
> THE HOLDS FOR ME

Exactly
(the top half was a cop out)
NOW the top is as good
as the bottom and it
makes a ~~good~~ route.
BETTER

OBVIOUSLY THE NO TOP ✗
HOLDS WILL BE CHALKED ROPE
ON A 2nd ascent straight ↗
after the first.

Try and repeat the
route before the comments ~~~~. John ~~~~

'Twas Phil Kelly who TRIED
to topRope it 2yrs ago (failed)(PK)

Page 72 coming soon

Anglezarke.

Shibb. *** 60' E3 6b.

Coal Measure Crag.

Takes the obvious line of weakness 20' L of Gritstone Rain. — Good line; Good climbing, Good rock.

15th Aug '83

Richard Toon
Mark Liptrot.

New Jerusalem *** 60' E4 6a.

Another brilliant route up the obvious line 20' left of Shibb. 1(p.r.).

25th Aug '83

Liptrot, Toon.

Give Thanks. 60' E4 ~~6b~~ 6a

Start beneath bolt holes on the wall R. of Samarkand. Climb easy rocks to the R until it is possible to gain the centre of the slab via a small projecting block. Up the slender groove/slab direct. Bold and fairly intense.

~~Dave Before~~, 22nd Aug '83

~~Phil Kelly~~: 1982. (MAROL) Liptrot / Toon.
though slightly different (p.r.)

✱ N.B.

Beware of imminent rock falls in Sleeper Bay area. Large block has slipped on Sleeper Bay causing the top 15' to be VERY unstable.

Aug '83. Dave Sanders

66

Central Ave.   VS 5c E3

   Climb wall wall right of
central crack to top. topwall crux.

         D. Bennett
          Sept 1976

Anglezark Quarry.

King of Kings. 75'   E5 6b.

   Start up Please hock the Away to the horizontal break; move up then climb the wall leftwards to a junction with Klondyke Up this to finish.

         17th March '84
           M Liptrot / D Vose.

   This route now finishes independently by swinging 'R' from the "good" holds and going straight up the wall. One poor peg removed, good peg runner in situ.

Very sustained   E5 6b.
          M Liptrot / B. Bradbury
           20th March '84

Cadshaw Quarry (Yarsdale).

Monkey Crack   E2 5c   free   M. Liptrot solo
                9/4/84

Marmoset   E2/3 6b/c   free
         M liptrot solo after self belaying.

Anglezark Qry.

   Gates of Perception. Direct finish.
Straight up the front face of the tower using the arrette and the thin crack. More sustained at E4 6a.
        M Liptrot / Dave Vose
          19/4/84

Transfered from shop book.

Angleszarke.

The Absent Minded Professor.   E3 5c,

Start 10' R. of Tangerine Trip. Climb the wall and move onto T.T. at its thin crack. Climb T.T. past the pod and move L and climb the wall swinging R to finish.

M. Liptrot / R. Toon   30/6/84

Parbold. Quarry.

K.A.M.   on Diamond wall.   40' V.S.

6' R. of Kamikaze Cuckoo. Long reach to ledge below large horizontal break. Climbs the wall directly finishing on L of O.H of Gillens Route.

D. M. Cross 16/8/84

327   H.V.S. 35ft.

5' L of Poverty, Poverty.

Climb the overhangs directly below large oak tree. Loose near the top!

D. M. Cross 16/8/84.

HOGHTON QUARRY

GREG RIMMER: THE MOTION PICTURE
E4 5c/6a

Start as for Slanting Crack.
Jimmy up S.C. and follow its
continuation flake till it is possible
to throw oneself L. to a good hold.
Extend LWDS (Gibsonism) to hold
in groove + power up to ledge.
Move L again to finish up
Sirloin to the Pasture.

MALC. HASLAM
RONNIE MARSDEN.

Parbold Quarry

"Fossil Alternative"
VS 4c (Direct start to Fossil Orig)
3ft L of "Fossil Orig". Direct over
overhang, continues on original route.
2/2/85   Steve Smith.

Anglezarke

Dancing on the Valentine. E2 5c
Start up Metamorphosis to the first
ledge + climb the wall above just L
of the arete.
15/2/85
M. Liptrot.

Agrajag   E3 6a.
Up the thin crack, R. of
Golden Tower start, to overlap. Move
L (runner in G.T.) Step back R
and go up centre of wall.
15/2/85
M. Liptrot.
P.T.O.

70

Parbold Quy.
"Main Wall Girdle"   HS. 4b   140'
1/ 40ft Start at "Bull", move diagonally
under large block to large ledge.
2/ Continue half hight across to corner
round to large ledge.
3/ Finish up "Lucky Grab."

                    S. Smith
                    A. Maxwell
                    A. Fisher.
                    Jan '85

※ N.B. KEEP OUT. (why)
Parbold Main Quarry only
finished production 5 years ago
and so is very dangerous. I
notice some routes have been
suggested but the general concensus
of oppinion is that it is far
too unstable for sensible climbers. The
owners also do not wish climbing to
take place for obvious reasons.
                        Dave Sanders

Complete catalogue of climbs from 7th Grade Book.

Lester Mill Qry.

16A. Whip Me! Whip Me!   Severe 20'

Top of grass covered cone left of "Twin Grooves". Climb right crack and top then over blocks. Top loose. Scrappy.

R. Bunyan. D. Sanderson.

Aug 82.

Anglezarke.

The Rapidity of Sleep   HVS 5c 40'

Again and climb the thin crack 10' R of 'Flake Out' with a technical start. Either abseil from a ledge 10' from the top or drop a rope from the top to facilitate topping out. Led with pre-placed nut then soloed.

Aug 82

Mark Liptrot.

Obiwan   E2 6a. 60'

Free climbs 'Havasupai'. Grade takes into account peg protection which has since be removed.

Aug '87

Mark Liptrot.

Wilton 1

Falling Wall   E1 5b   45'

20ft L of 'Willow Arete'. Climb the thin crack to the small ledge. Then climb the wall above.

Tim Lowe

Dave Vose.   19.5.83

Anglezarke

Turkish Delight   VS 5b.

Parallel line of flukes just L of 'Kebab' with a hard start. From the big ledge traverse L and finish

PTO.

'Elder Groove'

8/6/83

Mark Liptrot. (Solo).

* The route "Superb" in the new guide was climbed in 1980 by Mark Liptrot and Dick Toon and is called "Grand".

Lester Mill   The following routes are of little consequence.

Albert's Absolutely Amazing Eliminate   30' Severe.
The thin crack just L of "Newsam Slab" continue direct

M. Liptrot Solo.

Sidney's Supersonic Mega-Route   30' Severe
climbs R of 'Newsam Slab' past some "cemented on" holds and continue direct.

M Liptrot
Solo.

Inconceivably Mega Tronic.   30' MVS,
The corner from a big ledge just L of 'Small Oak Crack'

M. Liptrot Solo.

Gee a 5.11 off width.   30' VS.
The wall between the previous route and 'Small Oak' Topping out is the crux.

M. Liptrot Solo.
28.6.83

Pinnacle Problem.   40' Severe.
Start as for 'Left Twin Groove' 15' up climbs left crack of "pinnacle", stand on top and then up two walls above.

Nigel Bunyan. / Roge Bunyan.
July 83

Anglezarke

Elaine   HVS. 6a.

Boulder problem wall just left of 'Wedge', avoiding square cut hold on the right, From the break finish up the good crack on L.

20/7/83
M. Liptrot. Solo.

Vishnu (direct start).   E1 5c

The thin crack 10' R of the original start

31/7/83
M. Liptrot (Solo).

Mission Impossible   70'   E2 5b.

Up 'Terra Cotta' to break below roof. Traverse this L to 'First Finale' pull up L and finish as for 'Zarke'.   30/7/83   M.Liptrot, John Dodd.

Shibb *** 60'   E3 6b

Takes the obvious line of weakness 20' L of 'Gritstone Ruin'.

15/8/83

Dick Toon , M. Liptrot.

New Jerusalem *** 60'   E4 6a.

Another good route up the obvious line 20' L of Shibb. 1 peg runner.

25/8/83
Liptrot, Toon.

Give Thanks. * 60' E4 5c.

Start beneath the bolt holes on the wall R of 'Samarkand'. Climbs easy rocks to the R until it is possible to gain the centre of the slab via a small projecting block. Up the slender groove/slab direct. Bold and intense 22/8/83 Liptrot / Toon.

NB. Sleepo Bay Area is in a very dangerous condition.

KING. OF KINGS. *** 75' E5/6 6b/c.

Original Route ^(E5 6b.) Start up P.L.A. to the break. move up then climb the wall leftwards to a junction with Klondyke. Up this to finish.

17/3/84 Liptrot/Vose.

Direct ~~finish~~ E5 6b.
~~No Route~~ This route now finishes direct by swinging R from the "good" holds and going streight up the wall. One very poor peg (removed) and a good (insitu) peg runner en-route.

M. Liptrot, B. Bradbury.
20/4/84.

Direct Start. Makes rout totally independent.
Up crack left of P.L.A.   Ian McMullEn (crack only).
Complete route   M. Liptrot   25/9/84.

N.B. please do not remove pegs placed in this rout. M. Liptrot.

Cadshaw Qry   Yarsdale Delph

Monkey Crack   E2 5c. Free.
                       Mark Liptrot (solo).
Marmoset   E2/3 6b/c. Free.
                       M. Liptrot (solo) after self belaying.
                       13/4/84

Anglezarke   E4 6a.
    Straight up front face of Tower. using the arete
and the thin crack. More sustained.
                            M. Liptrot. D. Vose.
                                    19. 4. 84.

___

Wilton 2
    Against All Odds.   E5 6c.
    Climbs "S" groove by an all out smear move
and a decidedly thin layback.
                            H. Leach. 18/5/84.

___

Anglezarke.
The Absent Minded Professor   E3 5c
        Start 10' R of 'Tangerine Trip'. Climb the wall
and move onto 'Tangerine Trip' at its thin crack. Climb T.T.
past the pod and move L and climbs the wall
swinging R to finish
                            M. Liptrot, Dick Toon 30/6/84

___

Wilton 1
        The Thin Whiteline ** E3 6a   35ft.
    Climbs the obvious thin crack to the right of
White Slabs Bunt to the belay ledge. Finish as
for W.S.B.
                            Tim Lowe
                            Bernie Bradbury.   16.8.84

Chance Encounter **   30ft   E3 5c
        Climbs the diamond shaped buttress to the L
of Undertakers Crack. Peg runner at 25'.
                            Tim Lowe, Dave Vose,
                            Derek Kenyon.   16. 8.84

Parbold Qry.

<u>K.A.M.</u>   on. Diamond Wall.   40' VS.
        6' R of Kamikaze Cuckoo
   Long reach to ledge below large horizontal
Break.   Climb the wall directly finishing on
L of overhang on Gillen's Route.
                                16.8.84
                                    D. Cross.

<u>327.</u>   35' H.V.S
        5' L of Poverty Poverty.
   Climb the overhangs directly below large oak
tree . Loose near top .
                                16/8/84
                                    David Cross.

<u>The Grouse Beaters.</u>   H.V.S 30'
        4' R of "Soft Joe" climb thin cracks
direct through overhangs and step L at the tree.
                                29/8/84
                                    D. Cross
                                    R Stanley.

<u>Fossil Alternative</u>
        VS 4c   Direct Start to Fossil Original
3ft L of Fossil Original , Direct over overhang.
Continue up original route ,   2/2/85
                                    Steve Smith.

<u>Main Wall Girdle</u   HS. 4b.   140'
① 40' 3a Start a Buil. Move diagonally under large block
to large ledge above 'Sacrificial Block'. ② 4a Continue
at half hight across to corner round to large ledge. ③ 15' 4b
finish up 'Lucky Grab'. Steve Smith, Andrew Maxwell,
                              Andrew Fisher. Jan 85

WILTON TWO

PUSS & SOLDIERS

– ** ~~Puss Soldiers~~ E4 6b

START 4ft L OF SHALLOW GROVE ~~CORNER~~
GAIN ~~A~~ A BREAK AND HAND
TRAVERSE L (TO A) FINE CRACK.
SWAY UP THE CRACK to A MANTLE.
ARRANGE A THREAD RUNNER (CRUX).
~~So~~ DO a MEGA BODY SWERVE
AROUND ONTO THE BLUNT NOSE.
UNDERCUT THE OVER LAP TO
TOP. (NECKY)

A. GRIDS
S. SHARPLES   2/7/85

A Modern Classic Me ***

TIM LOWE climbed the wall R of JOSSER
at E4 6b but used a peg runner
as a side runner in an already established
vs. climb (FEARFULL FRANK). On making
the second acsent of this I eliminated
the side RUNNER and added a new
First Pitch (SOLO). still the original name

WELCOME TO THE PLEASURE DOME   E5
6b WALL L of First Pitch of (F.F), moving R
near the top P.P solo

6b THE wall R of ~~JOSSER~~ going R at
the top.

Paul Pritchard

2nd Ascent Jimmy N.P
E2/3c 6A
Mark Leach E6a V
REAL
Dreamer

HOGHTON

FALLOUT DIRECT START   E2 5c   **
    Start up New Wave, then get off it as
quickly as possible by moving left into a
flake/groove system which leads entertainingly
to an accomodating ledge. Either belay here
or continue up pitch 2 of Fallout.

            FA DAVE CRONSHAW. 9/8/83.
Going Straight for New Wave is better!
*** STOP PRESS (no grade) why!   R. Foster
    Houghton Quarry is now open
to rock climbers and is being
defoliated - if you go dont forget
   to NUKE some vege.   - Shitty doxorphin

            ← FRIGGED   PISS off
                    (Paul Heaton   PIGSHIT!

WILTON 1.

    JIMMY MAC - BIN MAN EXTRAORDINAIRE E25c, 4c.
                        Macklike E6a 2nd asc.
    Freeclimbs FGARFUL. FRANK. 1 PR. in Situ.
                    ? FROG?   TROG - Put the Peg
    Phil Kelly, Trog, Paul Pritchard.   BACK.

WILTON
"PROW
"RENAMED BORING PIECE"
OF SHIT   OVER HANGING FACE
Paul Wood   Left OF RAMBLING ROUTE

THE NELSON BULLSHIT PAGE

Wilton 3

BOLT BELAY

ORANGE SQUASH — Now reclimbed. Since the demise of the flake at E3 6a FA Paul Pritchard without Prejudice — I reclimbed this bag of shit as it was originally done but, Paul, why did ya not climb all the crack, ie; traversing level with the "Peg". until this line (or a more direct line) is climbed, the consensus of opinion in lancashire at this present time would suggest that you are a stupid little pratt, for claiming such a naff line as this, I mean who wants 16a more, Massive ledge, Reach Right and finish up 2 feet of a shit crack, until you realise that Comici was Right ("let a drop of water fall from the summit and that shall be my line"), you will never be respected as one of lancashire's greatest activists of all time after Hank Pasquil, Ian Lonsdale, Mark Leach, John Hartley, Dave Cronshaw and Phil Kelly (!!) Until such time as this we will consider you nothing but a frigging Pillock! We also remember "The gay dwarves and Mr Plod go to the tupperware Party" (The ball R. of Crooked Crack in Wilton 3) The loosest, dirtiest, shittest route in the world. finally a quote from Guru Lonsdale

"fuck off, Paul"

yours faithfully

PK (THE SEA CUCUMBER)

And in the words of Messner who wants to be a slave of the Plumline

PEG
RURP
POOR FRIEND 2
About as active as a SEA CUCUMBER

this was in my younger days when I was but a young man

at least I didn't rest on 'Loopy' 'JIMMY MAC' GOLDEN MOMENT. Central CK. fine time Pluto Salmon leap. Master Spy

Many, Many More (PK) eg. Insanity, Traffic Jam, Minister, John Peel. by the way, it's a classic route fingerswing Daytonawall, Left Hss. MeinKampf, L..yte L.H. Ann, Crater Traitor, Mi

ANGLEZARKE.

KING   OF   KINGS
The direct start makes
the route totally independant
Devastating E5/6 6b/c
complete Ian McMullen (crack only)
route
Mark Liptrot. 25/9/84

PLEASE NOTE - will the
person who nicked the pegs
out of the top wall please
not do it again or he'll
get he's knee caps broken.
                    Here, Here!

Parbold Quay.

    THE GROUSE BEATERS. H.V.S 30'
4 L. of 'Soft Joe' climbs thin cracks direct through
overhang and step L. at tree.
              29.8/84   D.M.CROSS
                             ROBIN.N. STANLEY

CLASSIFIED ADS.

CRAIGXLONGRIDGE — supercedes Brownstones AS THE
HARD mans Bouldering crag

Routes described from left to Right
AND ALL numbered at the bottom of the crag.
look out for new guide book
plenty of scope for new routes/problems
so come on lads get your thumbs out

A. GRIDLEY S. sharples P. Pritchard
T. GRIDLEY P. KELLY J. MARSDEN
To name but a few
dissatisfied visitors

ie:- MUSCLES IN THEIR IMAGINATION 6a*** The wall Loof weir Aardvark
gart g L. words   FA Phil Kelly '85

Here's what some visitors have said

" Is that it " Phil. Kelly.

" what a bag a choss Phil Garlick
I did these years ago."

" Im going back to the pub" A. GRIDLEY

" The most Dynamic crag
in Lancashire" PP

" What a load of Bull Shit"

GO SUCK PP

" Beware of low flying Gridleys "
Ron Fawcett who?

oh you dont
get better them
a M leach
frigger "boy"
he's the
that "Dogs
Bullshits
A. GRIDS
(there's an open
invitation to you to go
to the crag Mark)

CRONSHAWS CROP of 84

FARLETON CRAG
_____

20a   DIMPLE DIMPLE   HVS   5a/5b
Wall between Clayfire & Pudding Club.
                                    Dave Cronshaw.
_____

CADSHAW
_____

32a   IT'LL END IN TEARS   E1   5b
Wall between Allsopps Arete & Quarry Groove.
Starting at niche climb cracks to finish at large flake.

33a   SPILT MILK   severe
Line starting 10' right of Quarry Groove. Finish as
that route.
                              Dave Cronshaw John Ryder.
_____

HOGHTON
_____

93a   IN THE PINK   E1   5b 5c
Wall between Cirrhosis & Tia Maria.
Start up crack 6' left of T.M. to ledge. Finish
up thin crack in wall above.
                              Dave Cronshaw John Ryder.
_____

ROUNDBARN
_____

5a STARSAILOR   VS 4c
Up corner left of Pross to roof. Hand traverse
left & finish.
    RIGHT

5b GHOST DANCER   E1   5c   Hoo.
Between Starsailor & Pross there is a wall.
Up wall via a flake and sandy pocket.
                              Dave Cronshaw John Ryder

85

Roundbarn contd. (Boring Quarry)

At the quarry entrance, by the concrete blocks, the main track bears left past a ruined building. After about a 100 yards there are a ~~above~~ above hollows on the right. The most obvious of these is about 30' high with an easy corner on the ~~left~~ right.

i) FORBIDDEN FRUIT   E1 5c
~~Climb the~~ Left of the easy corner are twin cracks.
Climb the thin crack awkwardly.

ii) HOLE IN THE WALL   HVS 5b
Takes the centre of the wall to finish past high peg runner.

iii) GAY DECEIVER   H.S. 4b
The blunt arete on the left. (Geddit!?!)

Dave Cranshaw John Ryden.

Brownstones.

ENUBRIATED   5b

The KNIFE EDGE ARÊTE RIGHT OF BLURT
VARIANT . Using mega UNDERCUT.
~~DESPAT~~ ~~DESPEAD~~ ~~DESPA~~ BLOODY EXPOSED
could ~~take~~ MONSTER 3 FOOT LOB

WILTON 3   FORK CRACK VARIATION ***
         CLIMB IT IN THE SAME WAY IT'S BEEN
CLIMBED FOR 20 YEARS
              (PHIL KELLY MOVE)
                PHIL KELLY.

    NORMAL

BROADBOTTOM QUARRY.
CAR BOOT SALE   E3 6a   40ft.

(Climbs the overhanging wall ^NEXt to road. using the Arete to
the right   P.LUKE + D O'rourke

    Direct the free version of steeply cracks
proper without the arete. E4 6a/b.
                          John Bray (ZURCH)

free wheelin' franklin   45 ct   E3/4 6a.

The obvious scoop to the left of elder wall
Direct start and follow the scoop to the top
break then go left to the tree to avoid
loose rock.

                   John Bray solo LURCH
                      (after absail inspec-
                                      tion)

87

ISSA crag in the wood

SHOOTER NAB

Cursecure. 3O E4 6A
The right side of central crack
up for E4 goal to the
first good hole. Make some
Bosmoke moons on small
shales to the angle, they
follow this to the top
    Paul and Brian Cropper
        19/6 85

8A He Mode. HVS 5A
Follow the obvious arete
Direct
    Paul Cropper R. Siddiqui

47A Surprise. 40 H.V.S 5B.
Climbs the overhang wall
and scoop above, to the
slab and up this
     Paul Cropper G Gibson
        85

Yellowgate U.F.O. HVS 4C
climb the wall between
36 and 36.
    G Gibson. 84

The long Reach has had a 2nd Asc. after 8 years — 636b
    Paul Cropper, phil Kelly '85.

Chew Valley

Standing stones

Digital Dilemma E2 5c/6a   (Depending on how thick
                                your fingers, or the leader
                                are).
Climb the cracked overhanging wall left of Guillotine
to a thin crack left of the arête. Climb the
crack to the ~~ a r ê t e~~ arête and layback up it
to the top.
        N. Siddiqui   Con Carey, Paul Cropper
        7/7/82.

B. Chee Dale   LONG WAY FROM LANCASHIRE HILLS
                                              YOUTH
Moving Buttress

Protest and Survive 80' E3 6a

Climb a crack just left of Whistling crack
to a bulge. Move left with difficulty to
a poor peg runner. Make a hard move up to
a flake crack and continue to the break
(old thread runners on the girdle). Pull over the
bulge and finish slightly right.

    N. Siddiqui, Jim Moran, Geoff Milburn, Don Campbell
    11/7/82

EGERTON
                THE ICE COOL ACID TEST.   20/7/82
    80' XS 5B.

        Takes the wall the right of Alec Trench.
    Superb wall climbing. Peg runner at
    30 feet. Runner used in whiteout level
    with peg on Alec Trench.
        Dai Lampard. Nigel Holmes.

"A MAJOR BREAKTHROUGH IN BRITISH CLIMBING"
- chipped to perfection!
"I thought I was dead" → PETE LIVESEY
→ Ron Fawcett

Wilton 3

33 a) Between 33, 34 ✓   WHAT'S THIS?

The wall straight up exiting right at the top
Called = _caustic orange_ (E1, 5c)
                                        7b

(FROG paul wood), Gary Spindler 7/7/83
        THIS ROUTE IS BRILLIANT PHIL KELLY
                                (JOKE)
                                        HONEST!   FUTURE? ROUTE?

WILTON 2

"2 PVC GIRLS GO SLAP HAPPY" E5 6b

Climb direct to second peg of "IRON ORCHID". Step right
to second peg runner, then straight up the wall without
using Saturday Crack for holds or runners. a fall from near
the top would be serious.

CRAP

        First Ascent   Roland Foster (N2) 10/6/83

        Seconds - Greg Rimmer Mick Ryan
SOLOED BY MARK LEACH April '84

DENHAM

LOCK-OFF LOCOMOTION E1 5c
Starts up LH arete of wall under overhangs. Up to
roof, pull round & hand trav. L to arete. Move
up and ramble up to top. A bit of a pumpy bravete
                Matt Haslam / Greg Rimmer

JIMMY SIDEWAYS   HVS 5a
Start in corner R of Rockdancer. Trav R above
lip of overhang to rib which is followed to top.
                Rimmer / Mick Ryan / Haslam

CEASELESS TIDE   VS 5b
Between Midget + Fingerbone. Climb rib and wall. (Rib
gained from L.)
                Haslam

WILTON I ~~E3~~ H.S 8b/6a
GO UP THE WALL !

DESCRIPTION   GO UP THE BIG WALL
ON THE RIGHT.

Paul Mitchell solo astotop.

(CHAM FRANCE)   REACH FOR THE
SUPERMARKET   XS (10.12b) Rguns

PITCH ONE (6a).
DRESS IN CASUAL UNOBTRUSIVE
CLOTHS SO AS NOT TO BE SPOTTED.

PITCH TWO (3a).
Venture to the SUPERMARKET
AND PURCHASE PROTECTION
78 LITRES OF AMBER FALLING
DOWN LIQUID.

PITCH THREE (6c) CONSUME PROTECTION.

PITCH FOUR (-CRUX) (7a)

DRIVE VAN (GET AWAY VEHICAL) to
CHAM TOWN CENTRE ENSURING ENGINE
IS NICE AND WARM. PARK UP NEXT
TO STATUE OF TWO ~~bebe beet~~ chaps
pointing somewhere, leave back doors
open, and engin running, with van
pointing out of cham and to the
border.

Pitch FIVE (2b) Place two belayers at
good vantage points to acte as
lookouts.

Pitch SIX (6a) Climb cross the
lower bed to a minute stace
re bolts or pegs!

Pitch Seven (5a)

Mount the base buttress with diff.
(due p to protection consumer) and
climb direct to the two cheaps feet.

Pitch Eight. (7a)

climb out over the overhang using
delicate pinch gip on a testical.
and an awkward nipple squeeze.
to gain the right arm. Easy hand
traverse leads to obvious first finger

Pitch Nine (6b)

By swinging free ~~till~~ on one
hand that the finger with Ice
axe held in other hand until
either the finger bends or drops
off along with you.
Objective dangers are now encounter
ie local frogs awatened by loud
bonding sound breated by hollow
bronze resinating figure.

Pitch Ten (7c)

Run like Fuck !
AND DON'T LOOK BACK

Pitch Eleven (3a)

get a good solisitor.

1) ANYONE PTTING
COMMENT OW THIS
SHOULD EITHER
A REPEAT IT

B GET BANDED
INSTANTLY

First ascent   Don Willans   (broke it
Second   —"—   Pete GRADY.   (bent it
Piss Head → Geof HIBBERT   (towards the
                               supermarket)

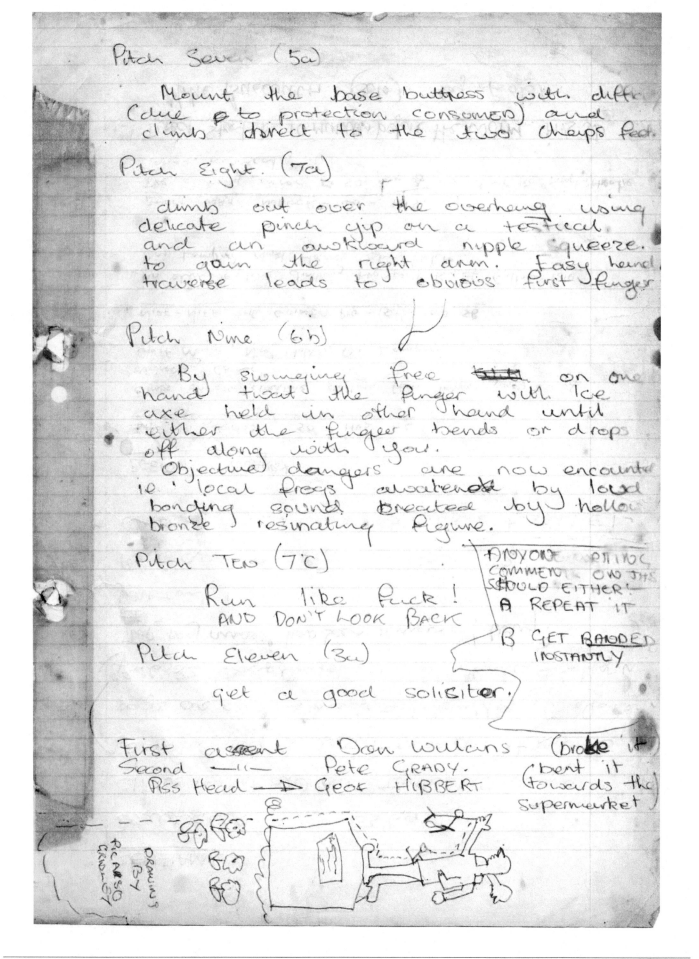

DRAWINGS BY
RICHARD CANDLET

Printed in Great Britain
by Amazon

31968473R00059